THE ULTIMATE
TURKEY FRYER
COOKBOOK

Over 150 Recipes for Frying Just About Anything

REECE WILLIAMS

Skyhorse Publishing

Skyhorse Publishing books may be purchased in bulk at special discounts for sales promotion, corporate gifts, fund-raising, or educational purposes. Special editions can also be created to specifications. For details, contact the Special Sales Department, Skyhorse Publishing, 307 West 36th Street, 11th Floor, New York, NY 10018 or info@skyhorsepublishing.com.

Skyhorse® and Skyhorse Publishing® are registered trademarks of Skyhorse Publishing, Inc.®, a Delaware corporation.

www.skyhorsepublishing.com

10 9 8 7 6 5 4 3 2

Library of Congress Cataloging-in-Publication Data is available on file.

ISBN: 978-1-61608-181-2

Printed in China

Chef Williams™, Chef Williams Marinades™, Chef Williams Original Cajun Seasoning™, and Chef Williams-Inventor of Injectable Marinades™ are registered trademarks of Chef Williams Foods LLC

Acknowledgments

First off, I'd like to thank my late father, Edgar Williams, for his lessons about innovation. Without his farsightedness, Cajun Injector® would have never happened. His spirit is still with me on every trip I take and every TV appearance I make. In a way, he's still teaching me.

"J. B.," my mom—that's short for Jeanne Belzons—taught me the basics of kitchen operation and design and how all that applied to the creation of recipes that went beyond the usual. What I got from my father in pushing the envelope perfectly complemented the firm foundation of what had gone before that I got from my mother. That's why together we all made a huge success of The Front Porch restaurant, then later Cajun Injector.

I'd also like to thank Mary, my wife, for sticking out the thin days when Cajun Injector didn't know how to grow except in fits and spurts. And in the middle of it all, she birthed four daughters and finished out a career as a Delta Airlines flight attendant. Those planes didn't need engines. All they needed was Mary.

Those who put the nuts and bolts together to get this cookbook up and running have my utmost respect, admiration, and sincere appreciation for their long hours, disheartening setbacks, and hot kitchens.

Muriel Williams, aka Wuzzie, my 3rd born of four daughters, helped me in the food business since she was 10 years old. She became so interested in the management side of my business, at the age of 12, she decided to "run" for the CEO. Thank God she settled for helping me in other areas. Muriel has been tremendous help at the Front Porch Restaurant (the birthplace of our injectable marinade business). She is now planning to begin her first year at LSU. Wuzzie has essentially taken on the entire edit job for the republication of this book. Many thanks to Wuz.

A big thanks also goes to research chef David Gallent. David is one of the nation's best chefs when it comes to fresh ideas in old pots. David's efforts to make this book come alive were nothing short of miraculous, and the recipes prove it. I know you'll enjoy them.

THE ULTIMATE TURKEY FRYER COOKBOOK

Introduction

The French Acadians who settled in southern Louisiana in the 18th century sure were an industrious and adventurous bunch. These people—whose descendants came to be known as Cajuns—didn't sit by the shore waiting for the latest shipment of spices from India. If something looked the least bit promising, whatever it was, it went POP—right into the mouth.

Fast-forward 200-plus years, and my family has pretty much that same spirit. That is, we figure if something tastes promising, it might even taste better fried. So POP—right into the fryer it goes. In fact, I trace the Deep Fried Turkey phenomenon back to the early 1950s when our family would fry up a couple of barnyard turkeys as part of the annual fall hog slaughtering tradition on my grandfather's farm about 80 miles north of New Orleans.

Who would have thought that fried turkey could get any better? But that's just what

happened in the late 1970s when my dad—an industrious food lover if there ever was one—created the injectable marinating process, bringing explosive flavor and irresistible juiciness to the bird using our Cajun Butter Recipe™ marinade. The Injectable Marinade business was born!

Soon we started selling our Cajun Injector® marinades and turkey fry kits in grocery stores from Houston, Texas, to Mobile, Alabama. And, food lovers down in Louisana, caught up in that same adventuresome spirit of the Cajuns who came before them, called and wrote with suggestions on how to use our new products for more than just frying turkeys.

Hence, over the years, we've tried a lot of other things fried. No doubt about it, we've fried up some winners! So go ahead—tap into your spirit of adventure and get to frying!

Dedication

This book is dedicated to my Dad, Edgar Williams, who, until his untimely death on November 8, 1995, was my closest friend, a great business partner, and the most hands-on teacher I ever knew. His love for humanity and desire to interact with everyone from the janitors to the CEOs, will always be an inspiration in my travels through life.

—Reece

A Little Bit of History...

My daddy, Edgar Williams, loved to cook from the moment he could hold a fork. He was born in historic Jackson, Louisiana, named for General and future President Andrew Jackson when he stopped by after the Battle of New Orleans. History and food surrounded Dad.

Dad soon made history himself by opening up Fried Chicken Log Cabins in three locations in and near Clinton, Louisiana. His sister Elaine remembers, "Mama (Veta Doughty) thought she'd died and gone to heaven. She loved fried chicken and ate it every other day. When Edgar opened his chicken places, she ate all the chicken she wanted without having to cook it or clean up!"

In 1977, Dad found a better way to make money doing what he loved best. He and my mom, Jeanne, and I opened The Front Porch restaurant a couple of miles south of Clinton. The eatery with its inviting front porch soon became a favorite as far south as New Orleans. People couldn't resist the taste of our concoctions of different spices and seasonings used as marinades on fried turkey, as well as prime rib, ribeye, and sirloin steaks.

But everything changed the day a group of friends showed up with a 20-pound beef roast they intended to cook for a company party. They begged us to use our secret ingredients to marinate the slab overnight. Dad immediately realized that his marinade would hardly penetrate the surface of such a large piece of meat in such a short amount of time.

He decided on the spot that we should inject the marinade. We headed for the local farmers' co-op feed and seed store and got a veterinarian's syringe used for inoculating horses and steers. Well, we "inoculated" that beef with our Cajun Au Jus and never looked back. We started injecting everything. Our juicy injected prime rib became so well known that The Front Porch was voted by the Louisiana Tourism Association as Best Restaurant in 1979.

Even after Dad sold The Front Porch in 1984, friends and relatives kept pestering us for jars of our marinades. The requests became so frequent, we found ourselves in Mama's kitchen every weekend just to keep up. Well, Mama soon tired of our mess in her kitchen and put her foot down with the suggestion that we build our own kitchen and start selling the marinades.

And so our injectable marinade business was born. We started selling our marinades in local convenience stores. A major buyer for Winn-Dixie supermarkets got hold of our marinade and fell in love with it. He put us in all the Winn-Dixies.

Soon after, we were recommended for a competition being sponsored by QVC (the national retail sales cable TV channel). Neither Dad nor I had ever heard of QVC, but everyone kept saying, "You gotta get on that show!" Well, Dad and I went on the show and introduced the idea of injecting marinades. We had six minutes to sell our allotted inventory—we sold out in 90 seconds! We soon became regulars at the studio, and our business grew substantially through the years.

In 1995, just as Dad and I were about to make another appearance on QVC, he developed chest pains and suffered a fatal heart attack at the studio. It was a real blow to me psychologically—I had traveled everywhere with Dad. We built the company together, discussed every idea together. Suddenly gone, my sounding board was gone. His laughter was gone too. It took me awhile to get over his absence.

But with the support of my family and friends, we have persevered, growing a very successful business. And—of course—our love of food!

Chapter I
FRYing Basics

Successful Deep FRYing

In order to get the food to the desired internal temperature when frying, high heat is needed. Fat and oil at high temperatures don't mix well with human physiology, so be sure you follow these safety tips.

• Use a pot, basket, and burner designed for deep-frying. It should be large enough to hold the turkey and enough oil to completely cover the turkey. (It can take up to 5 gallons of oil.)

• Do not overfill the fryer with oil. To estimate how much oil you need, before unwrapping the frozen bird, put it in the fryer; add water until the turkey is submerged. Remove the turkey and note the water level. This is the level your oil should reach.

• Have thermometers for taking oil and meat temperatures and long oven mitts on hand. Keep a fire extinguisher (appropriate for grease fires) nearby.

• Find a level dirt or grassy area on which to position the fryer. (Wooden decks are not appropriate; they can catch fire. Also, oil will stain concrete.) Do not fry your turkey indoors or in a garage or other attached structure.

• Only fry a turkey that is under 12 pounds.

• Thaw the turkey completely.

• Do not stuff the bird.

• Remove any plastic pieces from the turkey, such as a plastic tie to hold the legs together or the piece that pops up when the turkey is done. These plastics will melt in hot oil.

• Cook meat or poultry to the proper doneness. (See "Food-Safe Temperatures," page 13.)

• Keep children and pets away from the cooking area, and do not leave the hot oil unattended.

• Allow the oil to cool completely after use. Discard the oil by pouring it back into the original container using a funnel. If you plan to reuse the oil (only if the food cooked in the oil did not burn), strain it through 100-percent-cotton cheesecloth. Store in a covered container in the refrigerator. Reuse the oil once or twice within one month.

For more information, visit the National Turkey Federation Web site at www.eatturkey.com or call 202/898-0100, or call the USDA Meat and Poultry Hotline at 800/535-4555.

COOKING OIL OPTIONS

There are several types of oils that are great for deep frying. In general, choose an oil that is free of impurities. (Impurities in oil are what gives it a rich flavor and dark color. Impurities also cause the oil to smoke at a lower temperature.) Corn, peanut, soybean, canola, cottonseed, and safflower oils all work well for deep frying.

Common Oils and Smoke Points

Safflower oil . . . . 450°F
Cottonseed oil . . . . 450°F
Canola oil . . . . 437°F
Soybean oil . . . . 410°F
Peanut oil . . . . 410°F
Corn oil . . . . 410°F
Sunflower oil . . . . 392°F
Extra-virgin olive oil . . . . 250°F

ESSENTIAL EQUIPMENT FOR DEEP FRYING

Heavy gloves or oven mitts
Deep-frying thermometer
Instant-read or meat thermometer
Paper towels
Kitchen utensils such as tongs, meat fork,
    large slotted fry spoon, and/or fry basket
Plates or platters lined with paper towels
    (to drain fried foods after cooking)
Fire extinguisher

THERMOMETER KNOW-HOW

Use a deep-frying thermometer to check the temperature of the oil in the turkey fryer. This type of thermometer is made to measure extra-high temperatures.

To check the internal temperature of meat or poultry, use a meat thermometer or an instant-read thermometer. Both types should be inserted into the meat or poultry after it's removed from the hot oil. The instant-read thermometer will give a reading in seconds.

FOOD-SAFE TEMPERATURES

It's always a good idea to check the internal temperature of cooked meat and poultry to ensure correct doneness. Use the following temperatures from the U.S. Department of Agriculture as your guide.

Ground beef, pork, veal . . . . 160°F
Ground chicken and turkey . . . . 165°F
Whole chicken, turkey, duck
        or goose . . . . 180°F
Poultry breast . . . . 170°F
Poultry legs, thighs and wings . . . . 180°F
Fresh pork
        Medium . . . . 160°F
        Well Done . . . . . . 170°F
Fresh beef
        Medium rare . . . . . 145°F
        Medium . . . . 160°F
        Well done . . . . 170°F

How to Use the Chef Williams Original Marinade Injector

1. Attach needle to Chef Williams Original Marinade Injector by turning clockwise until snug. Do not overtighten the needle.
2. IMPORTANT: Be careful handling raw meat. Always pour marinade into a separate container before drawing it into the Injector. This will keep unused marinade from becoming contaminated.
3. Draw marinade into the Injector by pulling up the plunger.
4. For best results, insert Injector into the meat at different angles through the same hole. See illustration, right.
5. With both needle holes below the surface of the meat, push plunger down slowly while pulling Injector slowly out of the meat. This evenly distributes the seasoning.
6. Clean Injector with soap and warm water. Let it dry, and then lightly coat rubber tip of plunger with vegetable oil.

TURKEY

1. Remove giblets and rinse turkey. Drain cavity completely.
2. Inject turkey with a FULL Injector into points A, B, and C. See illustration, right.
3. Sprinkle outside of turkey generously with Chef Williams Original Cajun Seasoning seasoned salt, rubbing in well.
4. CAUTION: Make sure all water is drained from cavity before deep frying. Fry according to directions in "Successful Deep Frying," page 12, for $3\frac{1}{2}$ minutes per pound in 350°F oil.

CHICKEN

1. Remove giblets and rinse chicken. Drain cavity completely.
2. Inject chicken with a FULL Injector in points A and B and $\frac{1}{2}$ oz. into point C. See illustration, right.
3. Sprinkle outside of chicken generously with Chef Williams Original Cajun Seasoning seasoned salt, or paprika.
4. CAUTION: Make sure all water is drained from cavity before deep frying. Fry according to directions in "Successful Deep Frying," page 12, for 9 minutes per pound in 350° oil.

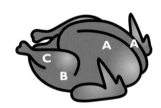

BEEF, PORK, AND WILD GAME

1. Inject 2 ounces of marinade per pound of meat at points every 1 to 2 inches apart. Use the technique described in "How to Use the Chef Williams Original Marinade Injector," above. On thick cuts of meat, inject from both sides.

Look for Chef Williams products in supermarkets and major retailers in the U.S. or visit ChefWilliams.com.

FRYing Times

	Minutes Per Pound	Oil Temperature*
Turkey, whole	3½	350°F
Turkey breast	7½	350°F
Turkey legs	8	350°F
Chicken, whole	8	350°F
Chicken breast	10	350°F
Cornish hens	8	350°F
Duck, whole	10	350°F
Pork loin	8	350°F
Leg of lamb, boneless	7 to 8	325°F to 350°F

Internal temperature should be at least 177°F.

Beef, prime rib	8	350°F
Beef, tenderloin	7 to 8	350°F

Use meat thermometer to test meat temperature for desired doneness.

Medium rare . . . . 145°F

Medium . . . . 160°F

Well done . . . . 170°F

Boiling temperature . . . . 212°F

*Note: It can take up to one hour to heat the oil to 350°F.

Chapter 2
Appe-FRYers

Hot Buffalo Wings

Ingredients

Oil
4 pounds chicken wings (about 20 wings)
1½ cups Chef Williams Cajun Butter Recipe
Chef Williams Original Cajun Seasoning

This fiery food originated in Buffalo, New York, where it was traditionally served with hot sauce, blue cheese dressing, and celery sticks. Down here in Louisiana, we like our wings on the spicy side. You may like them that way yourself.

COOKING INSTRUCTIONS

1 Preheat oil to 350°F.

2 Cut chicken wings apart at joints into 3 pieces; discard wing tips. Rinse chicken well with cold water; pat dry with paper towels. Inject each chicken piece with marinade; sprinkle with Chef Williams Original Cajun Seasoning.

3 Fry 10 to 12 wings at a time for 8 to 10 minutes or until golden. Remove from hot oil and drain on paper towels. Place hot chicken wings in a large bowl with additional marinade and toss well.

Serves 10 to 12.

Ingredients

Oil

3 pounds chicken wings (about 15 wings)

1½ cups all-purpose flour

1 tablespoon Chef Williams Original Cajun Seasoning

½ cup Chef Williams Cajun Butter Recipe

¼ cup cold butter, chopped

Blue cheese dressing

Sliced celery sticks

Chicken wings can be bought frozen, precut and a lot of times prebreaded. This saves time and mess. Be sure to thaw completely before frying.

COOKING INSTRUCTIONS

1 Preheat oil to 350°F.

2 Cut chicken wings apart at joints into 3 pieces; discard wing tips. Rinse chicken well with cold water; pat dry with paper towels.

3 Toss chicken wings in flour; shake off excess flour.

4 Fry 10 to 12 wings at a time for 8 to 10 minutes or until golden. Remove from hot oil and drain on paper towels. Combine Chef Williams Original Cajun Seasoning, marinade, and butter in a large bowl. Add hot wings; toss well until butter is melted. Serve with blue cheese dressing and celery sticks.

Serves 8 to 12.

Ingredients

- Oil
- ½ cup Chef Williams Cajun Butter Recipe
- 3 slices day-old bread, cut into 1-inch cubes (3 cups loosely packed)
- 2 pounds ground turkey or beef
- 3 large eggs, beaten
- ½ cup grated Parmesan cheese
- 1 tablespoon minced garlic Chef Williams Original Cajun Seasoning
- 2 teaspoons dried rubbed sage
- 1½ cups fine dry bread crumbs
- 1 teaspoon salt
- 2 cups barbecue sauce or Cajun Gravy (see page 155)

Lean ground beef, lean lamb, lean pork, or veal can be substituted for ground turkey.

COOKING INSTRUCTIONS

1 Preheat oil to 350°F.

2 Pour marinade over bread cubes; stir well. Let soak for 2 or 3 minutes. Break bread apart into small pieces. Add turkey, eggs, cheese, garlic, 2 teaspoons Chef Williams Original Cajun Seasoning, and sage; mix well. Shape mixture into 1½-inch balls.

3 Combine bread crumbs, 1 teaspoon Chef Williams Original Cajun Seasoning, and salt; stir well. Roll meatballs in bread crumb mixture, coating all sides well.

4 Fry 7 or 8 meatballs at a time for 4 minutes or until golden and cooked through. Remove from hot oil and drain well on paper towels. Toss meatballs in barbecue sauce or Cajun Gravy.

Serves 10 to 12.

Southwestern Egg Rolls

Ingredients

Oil
2 tablespoons butter
1 cup chopped red onion
1 cup finely chopped red sweet
    pepper
2 tablespoons seeded and
    minced jalapeño pepper
3 6-ounce skinless, boneless
    chicken breasts, cooked and
    chopped
1 cup canned yellow corn
1 cup canned black beans, rinsed
    and drained
2 teaspoons Chef Williams
    Original Cajun Seasoning
¾ teaspoon ground cumin
1 16-ounce package egg roll
    wrappers
1 large egg, well beaten
Salsa
Guacamole
Sour cream

COOKING INSTRUCTIONS

Egg rolls have been a favorite tailgating food of mine for many years. At an LSU game in 2000, the "Commissioner of Tailgating" Joe Cahn told me this recipe was one of the top finger foods he could remember trying. You may substitute pork, turkey, or shrimp if you prefer.

1 Preheat oil to 375°F.

2 Melt butter in a skillet over medium-high heat. Add onion, sweet pepper, and jalapeño; cook and stir 5 minutes. Remove from heat and let cool. Add chicken, corn, black beans, Chef Williams Original Cajun Seasoning, and cumin; mix well.

3 Spoon ⅓ cup filling in center of each egg roll wrapper. Fold top corner over filling, tucking tip of corner under filling; fold left and right corners over filling. Brush remaining corner lightly with egg; tightly roll filled end toward remaining corner and gently press to seal.

4 Fry 4 or 5 egg rolls at a time for 2 to 3 minutes or until golden, turning once. Remove from hot oil and drain on paper towels. Slice in half on a bias, if desired. Serve warm with salsa, guacamole, and sour cream.

Serves 16.

Black-Eyed Pea Fritters

Ingredients

- 2 tablespoons butter
- ¼ cup chopped red onion
- ¼ cup chopped red sweet pepper
- 2 green onions, finely chopped
- 3 cups cooked black-eyed peas, drained
- 1 large egg
- 2 tablespoons mayonnaise
- ½ cup fine dry bread crumbs
- 1 teaspoon garlic salt
- 1 teaspoon ground cumin
- 1 teaspoon hot sauce
- ½ cup cornstarch
- Oil
- Sweet Potato Relish (see page 141)

COOKING INSTRUCTIONS

As part of a world-wide tradition, having black-eyed peas (or some type of legume) on New Year's Day is a hope for good fortune. This fritter recipe takes black-eyed peas to a whole new dimension.

1 Melt butter in a small skillet over medium-high heat. Add onion and sweet pepper; saute 5 minutes. Add green onions; saute 2 minutes. Cool completely.

2 Coarsely mash black-eyed peas. Add onion mixture, egg, mayonnaise, bread crumbs, garlic salt, ground cumin, and hot sauce.

3 Shape mixture into 12 patties. Dust each patty lightly with cornstarch.

4 Chill 1 hour.

5 Preheat oil to 350°F.

6 Fry 3 or 4 fritters at a time for 3 to 4 minutes or until golden, turning once. Remove from hot oil and drain on paper towels. Serve warm with Sweet Potato Relish.

Serves 12.

Ingredients

- 2 tablespoons dark sesame oil
- 1 cup shredded carrot
- 1 cup thinly sliced shiitake mushrooms
- 1 cup snow peas, thinly sliced
- 1 teaspoon minced fresh ginger
- 1 teaspoon minced garlic
- 1 cup finely shredded green cabbage
- 2 green onions, thinly sliced
- ¼ cup Chef Williams Teriyaki Honey Recipe Oil
- 1 16-ounce package egg roll wrappers
- 1 large egg, well beaten

COOKING INSTRUCTIONS

1 Heat sesame oil in a skillet over medium-high heat. Add carrot, mushrooms, snow peas, ginger, and garlic; saute 5 minutes. Remove from heat; cool. Add cabbage, green onions, and marinade; mix well.

2 Preheat oil to 350°F.

3 Spoon ⅓ cup filling in center of each egg roll wrapper. Fold top corner over filling, tucking tip of corner under filling; fold left and right corners over filling. Brush remaining corner lightly with egg; tightly roll filled end toward remaining corner and gently press to seal.

4 Fry 4 or 5 egg rolls at a time for 2 to 3 minutes or until golden, turning once. Remove from hot oil and drain on paper towels. Slice in half on a bias, if desired. Serve warm.

Serves 16.

Ingredients

Oil
24 fresh whole jalapeño peppers
or 2 12-ounce jars whole
jalapeño peppers, drained
4 ounces Monterey Jack or
cheddar cheese, cut into
24 1½-inch-long strips
½ cup all-purpose flour
1 tablespoon Chef Williams
Original Cajun Seasoning
¾ cup buttermilk
Ranch-style dressing

*It's a good idea to wear rubber
gloves while handling hot peppers.*

COOKING INSTRUCTIONS

1 Preheat oil to 350°F.

2 Cut peppers lengthwise down 1 side, leaving the other side intact; remove seeds and membrane. Stuff each pepper with a piece of cheese.

3 Combine flour and Chef Williams Original Cajun Seasoning; stir well with a whisk. Slowly pour buttermilk into flour mixture while stirring; stir until smooth. Dip stuffed peppers in batter, coating all sides well.

4 Fry 6 to 8 peppers at a time for 2 minutes or until golden. Remove from hot oil and drain on paper towels. Serve warm with ranch-style dressing.

Serves 12.

Okra Poppers

Ingredients

- 40 medium-size okra
- 8 ounces pepper jack cheese, cut into 40 1½-inch-long strips
- Oil
- 3 cups finely crushed buttery crackers
- ¾ cup all-purpose flour
- 1½ tablespoons Chef Williams Original Cajun Seasoning
- 2 large eggs
- 1 cup half-and-half
- Ranch-style dressing
- Fresh salsa

COOKING INSTRUCTIONS

1 Rinse okra well with cold water; pat dry with paper towels. Cut okra lengthwise down one side, leaving the other side intact. Stuff each okra with a piece of pepper jack cheese.

2 Cover and chill 30 minutes.

3 Preheat oil to 350°F.

4 Combine crushed crackers, flour, and Chef Williams Original Cajun Seasoning; stir well with a whisk. In another bowl combine eggs and half-and-half; stir well with a whisk. Dredge okra in cracker mixture. Dip into egg mixture. Roll again in cracker mixture, coating all sides well.

5 Fry 6 to 8 okra at a time for 2 to 3 minutes or until golden. Remove from hot oil and drain on paper towels. Serve warm with ranch-style dressing and fresh salsa.

Makes 40 poppers.

Corn and Bacon Fritters

Ingredients

Oil

2½ cups all-purpose flour

2 tablespoons sugar

1 tablespoon baking powder

1 teaspoon salt

4 egg yolks

1 cup creamed corn

¾ cup milk

1 tablespoon hot sauce

1 16-ounce package bacon, cooked and crumbled

2 egg whites

These delicate fritters are great served as an hors d'oeuvre or with eggs and jam for breakfast.

COOKING INSTRUCTIONS

1 Preheat oil to 350°F.

2 Combine flour, sugar, baking powder, and salt; stir well with a whisk. In another bowl combine egg yolks, creamed corn, milk, and hot sauce; stir with a whisk until smooth. Combine flour mixture, egg mixture, and bacon; stir well.

3 In a clean bowl beat egg whites with a whisk until stiff peaks form; gently fold into batter.

4 Spoon batter by rounded tablespoonfuls into hot oil. Fry 4 or 5 fritters at a time for 4 to 5 minutes or until golden, turning once. Remove from hot oil and drain on paper towels. Serve warm.

Serves 10 to 12.

Cheese and Sausage Balls

Ingredients

- 2½ cups shredded sharp cheddar cheese
- 1 pound hot bulk sausage
- 5 cups packaged biscuit mix
- Oil
- 3 large eggs
- ½ cup milk

COOKING INSTRUCTIONS

1 Let cheese and sausage stand until room temperature. Reserve 1 cup biscuit mix. Combine cheese, sausage, 1 large egg, and 4 cups biscuit mix; mix well. Form mixture into 1½-inch balls; place on a cookie sheet lined with waxed paper. Cover and chill 2 hours.

2 Preheat oil to 350°F.

3 Combine the remaining 2 eggs and milk; beat well with a whisk. Dip balls into egg mixture. Roll in reserved biscuit mix, coating well.

4 Fry 8 or 10 balls at a time for 3 to 4 minutes or until sausage is fully cooked. Remove from heat and drain on paper towels.

Makes about 50 balls.

Sausage Wontons

Ingredients

Oil
1/2 pound ground sausage
2 teaspoons minced garlic
1 teaspoon minced fresh ginger
2 tablespoons minced green
    onion
1/2 teaspoon Chef Williams
    Original Cajun Seasoning
1/2 teaspoon ground red pepper
2 teaspoons cornstarch
1 ounce Chef Williams Teriyaki
    Honey Recipe
30 wonton wraps
Teriyaki sauce

COOKING INSTRUCTIONS

1 Preheat oil to 350°F.

2 Brown sausage in a skillet over medium-high heat; drain. Add garlic and ginger; cook 2 minutes, stirring constantly. Stir in green onion, Chef Williams Original Cajun Seasoning, and ground red pepper. Dissolve cornstarch in marinade; stir into sausage mixture. Cook 2 minutes over medium heat or until thickened. Set aside; cool completely.

3 Spoon 1 teaspoon of filling onto half of each wonton wrapper. Gently rub just a little water on edges of wonton wrapper until gummy. Fold 2 opposite corners together, forming a triangle; seal edges. Pull the left and right corners of folded triangle together so they slightly overlap. Moisten overlapping corners and pinch together.

4 Fry 6 or 7 wontons at a time for 2 to 3 minutes or until golden, turning once. Remove from hot oil and drain on paper towels. Serve with teriyaki sauce.

Serves 12 to 16.

Boudin Balls

Ingredients

- ¾ cup Chef Williams Original Roasted Garlic & Herb Recipe
- 2 teaspoons hot sauce
- 3 slices day-old bread, cut into 1-inch cubes (3 cups loosely packed)
- 2 green onions
- 3 garlic cloves
- 2 teaspoons Chef Williams Original Cajun Seasoning
- 1 teaspoon paprika
- 2 pounds boneless pork loin or boneless pork chops, cut into small pieces
- 3 large eggs, beaten
- 1 cup cooked rice
- 1½ cups finely ground buttery crackers
- 2 teaspoons salt
- Oil

COOKING INSTRUCTIONS

My uncle, Arch Doughty, was a sherriff of East Feliciana Parish for thirty-two years. He served this recipe at every election party (which could be why he won eight conecsecutive elections!).

1. Pour marinade and hot sauce over bread cubes; stir well. Let stand 10 minutes or until moisture is absorbed by bread. Process green onions, garlic, Chef Williams Original Cajun Seasoning, and paprika in a food processor until finely chopped. Add bread cubes; process until minced, stopping to scrape down sides with a rubber spatula. Spoon mixture into a bowl.

2. Process pork in a food processor until finely chopped. Combine bread mixture, pork, eggs, and rice; mix well. Shape mixture into 1½-inch balls. Combine crackers and salt; stir well. Roll pork balls in cracker crumb mixture, coating all sides well. Place pork balls on a baking sheet; refrigerate 1 hour.

3. Preheat oil to 350°F.

4. Fry 7 or 8 balls at a time for 4 to 6 minutes or until golden and cooked through. Remove from hot oil and drain on paper towels.

Serves 10 to 12.

Andouille au Fromage

Ingredients

Oil
3 tablespoons butter, melted
3 tablespoons all-purpose flour
2 cups milk
1 tablespoon Creole mustard
1 teaspoon hot sauce
1 teaspoon salt
2 cups (8 ounces) shredded
    cheddar cheese
2 1-pound packages smoked
    andouille sausage
Wooden toothpicks
1¾ cups packaged biscuit mix
1 tablespoon Chef Williams
    Original Cajun Seasoning
1 12-ounce ice cold beer

Andouille is a Cajun-style sausage. In this recipe it is sliced, battered, fried, and drizzled with a cheddar cheese sauce.

COOKING INSTRUCTIONS

1 Preheat oil to 350°F.

2 Stir together melted butter and flour in a heavy saucepan over medium-low heat; cook 2 minutes, stirring constantly. Slowly pour in milk; stir well. Cook over medium heat 3 minutes or until thickened, stirring constantly. Add mustard, hot sauce, and salt; stir well. Add cheese; stir until cheese melts. Set aside and keep warm.

3 Cut andouille into ¾-inch slices; pierce each andouille slice with a toothpick. Combine biscuit mix and Chef Williams Original Cajun Seasoning; stir well with a whisk. Add beer; stir until smooth.

4 Dip each andouille slice into batter. Fry a few slices at a time for 2 to 3 minutes or until golden, turning once. Remove from hot oil and drain on paper towels. Drizzle with cheese sauce.

Serves 12 to 16.

Bite-Size Crab Cakes

Ingredients

Oil
1 pound fresh or frozen lump crabmeat
½ cup fine dry bread crumbs
1 tablespoon crushed dried parsley
½ teaspoon salt
½ teaspoon black pepper
¼ cup mayonnaise
1 large egg, lightly beaten
2 teaspoons Chef Williams Cajun Garlic Recipe
1 teaspoon prepared mustard
Cocktail sauce (optional)

Lump crabmeat is expensive because it takes a lot of crabs to make a pound of it, but the extra cost is worth it. If you prefer, you can substitute claw meat.

COOKING INSTRUCTIONS

1 Preheat oil to 350°F.

2 Thaw crabmeat if frozen. Remove any shell pieces from crabmeat. Rinse crabmeat; pat dry with paper towels. Lightly squeeze to drain excess moisture; transfer to dish, cover, and chill until needed.

3 Combine bread crumbs, parsley, salt, and pepper; stir well with a whisk. Add mayonnaise, egg, marinade, and mustard; stir well. Gently stir in crab meat. Shape mixture into twenty-four 1-inch patties.

4 Fry patties in 2 batches for 2 minutes or until golden. Remove from hot oil and drain on paper towels. Serve warm with cocktail sauce, if desired.

Serves 8 to 12.

Bacon-Wrapped Oysters

Ingredients

Oil
2 quarts (4 to 5 dozen) fresh
    shucked oysters
1½ packages (16 ounces) smoked
    bacon
Wooden toothpicks
2 cups cornmeal
2 tablespoons Chef Williams
    Original Cajun Seasoning

COOKING INSTRUCTIONS

Smoked Bacon is essential to this recipe. You'll enjoy the best of both worlds—fried and smoked!

1 Preheat oil to 350°F.

2 Drain oysters; reserve liquor for other uses. Cut each bacon strip into thirds. Wrap each oyster with a piece of bacon. Secure with a wooden toothpick. Combine cornmeal and Chef Williams Original Cajun Seasoning; stir well with a whisk. Dredge oysters in cornmeal mixture, coating all sides well. Refrigerate until ready to fry.

3 Fry a few oysters at a time for 1½ to 2 minutes or until bacon is crisp. Remove from hot oil and drain on paper towels.

Makes about 4 dozen.

Shark Bites

Ingredients

Oil

¾ cup all-purpose flour

¾ cup cornstarch

2 teaspoons salt

¾ teaspoon white pepper

2 large eggs

¾ cup buttermilk

2 pounds fresh or frozen shark or
swordfish steaks, cut into
1½-inch pieces

Wasabi Marmalade (see
page 136)

COOKING INSTRUCTIONS

1 Preheat oil to 350°F.

2 Combine flour, cornstarch, salt, and pepper; stir well with a whisk. In another bowl combine eggs and buttermilk; beat well with a whisk. Thaw shark, if frozen. Rinse shark; pat dry with paper towels. Dredge shark pieces in flour mixture; shake off excess. Dip into egg mixture. Dredge again in flour mixture.

3 Fry a few slices at a time for 3 to 5 minutes or until golden. Remove from hot oil and drain on paper towels. Serve warm with **Wasabi Marmalade**.

Serves 4 to 8.

Zesty Fried Frog Legs

Ingredients

4 pounds frog legs
 Chef Williams Cajun Butter
 Recipe
 Oil
1 5½-ounce package zesty
 Italian-style croutons
2 large eggs
½ cup milk
 Williams' House Tartar Sauce
 (see page 144)

COOKING INSTRUCTIONS

Here in Louisiana, frogs are plentiful. It's no big deal to go frog hunting and catch an onion sack full of frogs.

1 Cut off feet of frog legs; discard. Freeze legs 30 minutes. Beginning at the top and working down, peel off skin. Rinse well with cold water; pat dry. Inject each frog leg with approximately 1 ounce marinade. Freeze 10 more minutes.

2 Preheat oil to 350°F.

3 Process croutons in a food processor until finely ground or place in a heavy-duty plastic bag; squeeze air out and crush with meat mallet or rolling pin. Combine eggs and milk; beat well with a whisk. Dip frog legs in egg mixture. Roll in crushed croutons, coating well on all sides.

4 Fry 8 or 10 legs at a time 3 to 4 minutes or until golden, turning once. Remove from hot oil and drain on paper towels. Serve with Williams' House Tartar Sauce.

Serves 10 to 12.

Bacon-Wrapped Artichokes

Ingredients

COOKING INSTRUCTIONS

Oil
2 14-ounce cans artichoke hearts
1 12-ounce package smoked
   bacon
Wooden toothpicks

Don't forget to use *smoked* bacon. **Not only does it add a great smoky flavor, but it also makes for a beautiful presentation.**

1 Preheat oil to 350°F.

2 Drain artichokes well. Quarter large artichokes; cut smaller ones in half. Cut each bacon strip into thirds. Wrap each artichoke with a piece of bacon. Secure with a wooden toothpick.

3 Fry a few artichokes at a time for 1½ to 2 minutes or until bacon is crisp. Remove from hot oil and drain on paper towels.

Makes about 4 dozen.

Nut-Crusted Brie

Ingredients

- 1 15-ounce round Brie cheese
- ¼ cup unsalted slivered almonds
- ½ cup unsalted pecan pieces
- ½ cup unsalted walnut pieces
- 3 tablespoons sesame seeds
- 2 tablespoons fine dry bread crumbs
- 1½ teaspoons salt
- 2 large eggs
- 2 large egg yolks
- ⅓ cup buttermilk
-   Oil
-   Hot pepper jelly
-   Crackers

COOKING INSTRUCTIONS

Gaye Sandoz, my sister-in-law and a very talented food stylist and cookbook author, developed this sweet and savory recipe. It's a favorite of mine for holiday parties.

1 Cut Brie into 8 wedges with a sharp knife. Cover and freeze 30 minutes.

2 Process almonds, pecans, and walnuts in a food processor until finely ground. Stir in sesame seeds, bread crumbs, and salt; set aside. Combine eggs, egg yolks, and buttermilk; stir well with a whisk.

3 Dip Brie wedges in egg mixture. Roll in nut mixture, coating all sides well. Cover and freeze 20 minutes.

4 Preheat oil to 325°F.

5 Fry 2 wedges at a time for 2 to 3 minutes or until crust is golden, turning once. Remove from hot oil and drain on paper towels. Serve warm with hot pepper jelly and crackers.

Serves 8 to 10.

Italian Fried Ravioli

Ingredients

Oil
1 5½-ounce package zesty
    Italian-flavor croutons
2 large eggs
½ cup milk
2 9-ounce packages refrigerated
    four-cheese ravioli
Marinara Sauce (see page 152)

COOKING INSTRUCTIONS

1 Preheat oil to 375°F.

2 Process croutons in a food processor until finely ground or place in a heavy-duty plastic bag, squeezing air out, and crush finely with meat mallet or rolling pin. Combine eggs and milk; beat well with a whisk. Dip ravioli in egg mixture. Roll ravioli in crushed croutons, coating well on all sides.

3 Fry 8 or 10 ravioli at a time for 2 to 3 minutes or until golden, turning once. Remove from hot oil and drain on paper towels. Serve with Marinara Sauce.

Serves 10 to 12.

Fried Walnuts

Ingredients

Oil
1 pound walnut halves
½ cup firmly packed brown sugar
½ teaspoon salt
½ teaspoon ground nutmeg
⅛ teaspoon ground cloves

In this recipe, the walnut halves are quickly flash-boiled to remove a negative flavor. They are then flash-fried in a lower temperature oil. Due to the high fat content within the walnut, frying for a longer period of time will burn the walnut and oil. Use only walnut halves because the walnut pieces will burn easily.

COOKING INSTRUCTIONS

Try this totally new and different recipe for your holiday snacks.

1 Preheat oil to 310°F.

2 Bring 2 quarts water to a boil in a 4-quart saucepan. Add walnuts and simmer 1 minute. Drain and place walnuts in a large bowl. Add sugar and toss well.

3 Fry walnuts in batches for 1 to 2 minutes.

4 Remove from hot oil and drain on a food rack positioned over paper towels. Cool completely. Toss with salt, nutmeg, and cloves.

Makes 1 pound.

Fried String Cheese

Ingredients

- ½ cup all-purpose flour
- 1 teaspoon salt
- 3 large eggs, beaten
- ½ cup milk
- 2 12-ounce packages mozzarella string cheese sticks
- 2 cups Italian-seasoned bread crumbs
- Oil
- Marinara Sauce (see page 152)

COOKING INSTRUCTIONS

1 Combine flour and salt; stir well with a whisk. In another bowl combine eggs and milk; stir well with a whisk. Dredge string cheese in flour mixture shaking off excess. Dip in egg mixture. Roll in bread crumbs, coating well on all sides.

2 Cover and chill 1 hour.

3 Preheat oil to 350°F.

4 Fry 4 or 5 sticks at a time for 2 to 3 minutes or until golden, turning once. Remove from hot oil and drain on paper towels. Serve warm with Marinara Sauce.

Serves 12.

Fried Dill Pickles

Ingredients

Oil

1 32-ounce jar sliced dill pickles

2 cups cornmeal

1 tablespoon Chef Williams
   Original Cajun Seasoning

COOKING INSTRUCTIONS

The vegetable dip on page 135 gives this recipe a really nice balance. This was a favorite snack food at "The Back Porch." The Back Porch was an oyster bar/waiting area at the first "Front Porch" restaurant we opened in 1977.

1 Preheat oil to 350°F.

2 Drain pickles well (use reserved pickle juice as a marinade for chicken, pork, or alligator). Combine cornmeal and Chef Williams Original Cajun Seasoning in a large heavy-duty plastic bag. Add pickles to cornmeal mixture; seal bag and shake well.

3 Fry a handful of pickles at a time in hot oil for 1½ minutes or until golden. Remove from hot oil and drain on paper towels.

Serves 10 to 12.

Bacon-Wrapped Olives

Ingredients

Oil
2 10-ounce jars garlic-stuffed jumbo olives
1 12-ounce package smoked bacon
   Wooden toothpicks

COOKING INSTRUCTIONS

1 Preheat oil to 350°F.

2 Drain olives; reserve juice for other uses. Cut each bacon strip into thirds. Wrap each olive with a piece of bacon. Secure with a wooden toothpick.

3 Fry a few olives at a time for 1½ to 2 minutes or until bacon is crisp. Remove from hot oil and drain on paper towels.

Makes about 4 dozen.

Home-Fried Tortilla Chips

Ingredients

Oil

1 25-ounce package 8-inch corn
   tortillas

Chef Williams Original Cajun
   Seasoning or salt

Fresh Tomato Salsa (see
   page 138)

After tasting the fresh flavor of just-fried corn chips, you won't want to go back to the bagged variety.

COOKING INSTRUCTIONS

1 Preheat oil to 350°F.

2 Cut tortillas into quarters. Fry a handful of chips at a time for 1 minute or until golden, turning once. Remove from hot oil and drain on paper towels. Sprinkle with Chef Williams Original Cajun Seasoning.

3 Serve with Fresh Tomato Salsa.

Serves 12 to 16.

Crispy Onion Straw-Blossom

Ingredients

Oil
½ cup sour cream
¼ cup chunky salsa
2 large (12 ounces each) white or Vadalia onions
¾ cup all-purpose flour
2 tablespoons chili powder
1 tablespoon garlic salt
1 teaspoon black pepper
1 cup all-purpose flour
¼ cup cornstarch
1 teaspoon salt
1 12-ounce beer

COOKING INSTRUCTIONS

1 Preheat oil to 375°F.

2 For sauce, combine sour cream and salsa in a small bowl. Refrigerate until serving.

3 To make onion flower, peel onions and cut ¾ inch off top of each onion. Trim, but do not cut off root end. Cut each onion into quarters from the top to ½ inch from root end. Then cut each quarter section into 4 thin wedges, cutting to within ½ inch from root end. Using a sharp knife, remove some of the center petals, careful not to cut through the bottom. Discard the center petals. Carefully spread the remaining petals apart.

4 Place the ¾ cup flour, chili powder, garlic salt, and pepper in a large heavy-duty plastic bag; add onion, shaking to coat. Shake off excess flour mixture. Repeat with the remaining onion.

5 Whisk the 1 cup flour, cornstarch, salt, and beer in a medium bowl until smooth. Dip onions in beer mixture, moving so onions are thoroughly coated. Drain to remove excess coating.

6 Using a long-handled slotted spoon or a wire basket, lower 1 onion, root-end side down, into hot oil. Fry about 3 to 4 minutes or until golden brown and onion is tender. Drain on wire rack. Spoon sauce into center of onion; serve immediately.

Serves 6 to 8.

Chapter 3
Turkey FRYs

Cajun Fried Turkey

Ingredients

Oil
1 10- to 12-pound fresh or frozen turkey
1 16-ounce jar Chef Williams Cajun Butter Recipe
Chef Williams Original Cajun Seasoning

Chef Reece Williams and his father, Edgar Williams, pioneered the concept of frying turkeys and invented their first turkey marinade, Creole Butter Recipe. This marinade has made the Cajun Fried Turkey a legend around the country.

COOKING INSTRUCTIONS

1 Preheat oil to 350°F.

2 Completely thaw turkey. Remove giblets and neck; reserve for other uses. If present, remove and discard plastic leg holder and pop-up timer. Rinse turkey well with cold water; drain cavity. Dry turkey well with paper towels. Pull the neck skin to the back and twist wing tips to the back holding the skin in place. Tuck the legs under the band of skin or tie legs to tail with cotton string.

3 Inject ½ cup marinade into each side of breast. Inject ¼ cup marinade into each leg and thigh. Sprinkle turkey with Chef Williams Original Cajun Seasoning.

4 Place turkey, breast side up, in basket. Slowly lower basket into hot oil, slowly; be cautious of splattering oil. Maintain oil temperature around 350°F. Fry turkey for 3½ minutes per pound. Remove from hot oil to check doneness. Insert an instant-read thermometer in the meaty part of the thigh; it is done when it reads 180°F. Remove from hot oil and drain on paper towels. Let rest 15 minutes. Carefully carve with a sharp knife.

Serves 8 to 10.

Deep Fried Turkey Breast

Ingredients

Oil

1 6- to 8-pound whole bone-in
    turkey breast

Chef Williams Cajun Butter
    Recipe

Chef Williams Original Cajun
    Seasoning

This is great alternative when you want fried turkey, but something a little smaller.

COOKING INSTRUCTIONS

1 Preheat oil to 350°F.

2 Rinse turkey well with cold water; pat dry with paper towels. Inject turkey throughout breast using 1 to 2 ounces marinade per pound of meat. Sprinkle with Chef Williams Original Cajun Seasoning.

3 Place breast in basket and lower slowly into hot oil. Fry breast for 8 minutes per pound. Remove from hot oil to check doneness. Insert an instant-read thermometer in the meaty part of the thigh; it is done when it reads 170°F.

4 Remove from hot oil and drain on paper towels.

Serves 8 to 10.

Ingredients

Oil
1 10- to 12-pound fresh or frozen turkey
2 tablespoons chopped fresh rosemary
2 tablespoons chopped fresh sage
2 tablespoons chopped fresh thyme
Cranberry-Ginger Sauce
Salt
Black pepper

Cranberry-Ginger Sauce
1 package (12 ounces) fresh or frozen cranberries
1 cup dried sweetened cranberries
1 cup apple juice
1 cup packed brown sugar
2 tablespoons grated fresh ginger

COOKING INSTRUCTIONS

1 Preheat oil to 350°F.

2 Completely thaw turkey. Remove giblets and neck; reserve for other uses. If present, remove and discard plastic leg holder and pop-up timer. Rinse well with cold water; drain cavity. Dry turkey well with paper towels. Slip your fingers between skin and meat to loosen skin over breast area. Lift skin, and press rosemary, sage, and thyme under the skin. Pull the neck skin to the back and twist wing tips to the back, holding the skin in place. Tuck the legs under the band of skin or tie legs to tail with cotton string.

3 Place turkey, breast side up, in basket. Slowly lower basket into hot oil; be cautious of splattering oil. Maintain oil temperature around 350°F. Fry turkey for 3½ minutes per pound. Remove from hot oil to check doneness. Insert an instant-read thermometer into the meaty part of the thigh; it is done when it reads 180°F. Remove from hot oil and drain on a wire rack. Let rest 15 minutes.

4 For Cranberry-Ginger Sauce, combine fresh or frozen cranberries, dried cranberries, apple juice, brown sugar, and ginger in a medium saucepan. Bring to a boil. Reduce heat and simmer 10 to 15 minutes.

5 Meanwhile, carve turkey; season with salt and pepper. Serve turkey with sauce.

Serves 8 to 10.

Maple Mustard Pecan Glazed Turkey

Ingredients

Oil

1   10 to 12-pound fresh or
     frozen turkey

1/4 cup maple syrup

3   tablespoons butter

2   tablespoons country-style
     Dijon mustard

2   tablespoons whiskey

1/4 cup finely chopped pecans,
     toasted

Salt

Black pepper

COOKING INSTRUCTIONS

1 Preheat oil to 350°F.

2 Completely thaw turkey. Remove giblets and neck; reserve for other uses. If present, remove and discard plastic leg holder and pop-up timer. Rinse well with cold water; drain cavity. Dry turkey well with paper towels. Pull the neck skin to the back and twist wing tips to the back, holding the skin in place. Tuck the legs under the band of skin or tie legs to tail with cotton string.

3 Place turkey, breast side up, in basket. Slowly lower basket into hot oil; be cautious of splattering oil. Maintain oil temperature around 350°F. Fry turkey for 3 1/2 minutes per pound.

4 Meanwhile, for glaze, combine maple syrup, butter, mustard, whiskey, and pecans in a small saucepan. Bring to a boil. Reduce heat and simmer for 2 to 3 minutes.

5 Remove turkey from hot oil to check doneness. Insert an instant-read thermometer into the meaty part of the thigh; it is done when it reads 180°F. Remove from hot oil and drain on a wire rack. Spoon glaze over hot turkey. Let rest 15 minutes. Carve. Season with salt and pepper.

Serves 8 to 10.

Ingredients

Oil

1 10- to 12-pound fresh or frozen turkey

2 small lemons

2 teaspoons dried oregano leaves, crushed

¼ teaspoon freshly ground black pepper

4 large cloves garlic, thinly sliced
Salt
Black pepper

6 medium (about 2½ pounds) russet potatoes, cut lengthwise into wedges

1 tablespoon peanut or vegetable oil

½ cup fine dry seasoned bread crumbs
Cucumber ranch dressing (optional)

COOKING INSTRUCTIONS

1 Preheat oil to 350°F.

2 Completely thaw turkey. Remove giblets and neck; reserve for other uses. If present, remove and discard plastic leg holder and pop-up timer. Rinse well with cold water; drain cavity. Dry turkey well with paper towels. Cut 1 lemon crosswise into thin slices. Cut remaining lemon into wedges; reserve until serving. Sprinkle each lemon slice with oregano and pepper. Slip your fingers between skin and meat to loosen skin over breast area. Lift skin and carefully tuck lemon slices and garlic under the skin. Pull the neck skin to the back and twist wing tips to the back holding the skin in place. Tuck the legs under the band of skin or tie legs to tail with cotton string.

3 Place turkey, breast side up, in basket. Slowly lower basket into hot oil; be cautious of splattering oil. Maintain oil temperature around 350°F. Fry turkey for 3½ minutes per pound. Remove from hot oil to check doneness. Insert an instant-read thermometer into the meaty part of the thigh, it is done when it reads 180°F. Remove from hot oil; drain on a wire rack. Let rest 15 minutes.

4 Toss potato wedges with 1 tablespoon oil; then with bread crumbs. Fry potatoes for 5 minutes or until brown and crisp. Remove and drain on a wire rack.

5 Squeeze reserved lemon wedges over turkey. Carve. Season with salt and pepper. Serve turkey with potato wedges and cucumber ranch dressing, if desired.

Serves 8 to 10.

Romano Turkey with Pesto Cream

Ingredients

Oil

1 10- to 12-pound fresh or frozen turkey

1 container (7 ounces) refrigerated basil pesto sauce

1 tablespoon butter

1 clove garlic, minced

1/2 cup fine dry seasoned bread crumbs

1/3 cup freshly grated Romano or Parmesan cheese

2 tablespoons finely chopped fresh flat-leaf parsley

1 cup sour cream

COOKING INSTRUCTIONS

1 Preheat oil to 350°F.

2 Completely thaw turkey. Remove giblets and neck; reserve for other uses. If present, remove and discard plastic leg holder and pop-up timer. Rinse well with cold water; drain cavity. Dry turkey well with paper towels. Slip your fingers between skin and meat to loosen skin over breast area. Lift skin and spread 1/4 cup pesto sauce under the skin. Pull the neck skin to the back and twist wing tips to the back, holding the skin in place. Tuck the legs under the band of skin or tie legs to tail with cotton string.

3 Place turkey, breast side up, in basket. Slowly lower basket into hot oil; be cautious of splattering oil. Maintain oil temperature around 350°F. Fry turkey for 3½ minutes per pound.

4 Meanwhile, melt butter with garlic in a large nonstick skillet over medium low heat. Add crumbs and cook until crumbs are lightly toasted, about 5 minutes, stirring frequently. Remove from heat. Stir in cheese and parsley; reserve.

5 Stir together remaining basil pesto sauce and sour cream in a small bowl.

6 Remove turkey from hot oil to check doneness. Insert an instant-read thermometer into the meaty part of the thigh, it is done when it reads 180°F. Remove from hot oil; drain on a wire rack. Sprinkle crumb mixture over turkey. Let rest 15 minutes. Carve. Serve with sour cream mixture.

Serves 8 to 10.

Tailgate Turkey & Onion Rings

Ingredients

Oil

1 10- to 12-pound fresh or
   frozen turkey

1 medium yellow onion, cut into
   ¼-inch slices

2 tablespoons beer

2 tablespoons honey

2 tablespoons country-style
   Dijon mustard

1 teaspoon chopped fresh
   thyme leaves

Onion Rings (see page 129)

COOKING INSTRUCTIONS

1 Preheat oil to 350°F.

2 Completely thaw turkey. Remove giblets and neck; reserve for other uses. If present, remove and discard plastic leg holder and pop-up timer. Rinse well with cold water; drain cavity. Dry turkey well with paper towels. Slip your fingers between skin and meat to loosen skin over breast area. Lift skin and carefully tuck onion slices under the skin. Pull the neck skin to the back and twist wing tips to the back, holding the skin in place. Tuck the legs under the band of skin or tie legs to tail with cotton string.

3 Place turkey, breast side up, in basket. Slowly lower basket into hot oil; be cautious of splattering oil. Maintain oil temperature around 350°F. Fry turkey for 3½ minutes per pound.

4 Meanwhile, combine beer, honey, mustard, and thyme in a small bowl.

5 Remove turkey from hot oil to check doneness. Insert an instant-read thermometer into the meaty part of the thigh; it is done when it reads 180°F. Remove from hot oil and drain on a wire rack. Spoon beer mixture over hot turkey. Let rest 15 minutes.

6 Carve turkey. Serve turkey with Onion Rings.

Serves 8 to 10.

Ingredients

Oil
1 10- to 12-pound fresh or
    frozen turkey
1 tablespoon orange zest
2 large cloves garlic, minced
¼ teaspoon ground red pepper
1 small onion, thinly sliced
   Orange-Cranberry Sauce

Orange-Cranberry Sauce
3 tablespoons butter
2 cloves garlic, minced
2 teaspoons curry powder
⅛ teaspoon ground red pepper
1¼ cups chicken broth
¾ cup frozen orange juice
    concentrate
⅓ cup dried sweetened
    cranberries
1 teaspoon cornstarch

COOKING INSTRUCTIONS

1 Preheat oil to 350°F.

2 Completely thaw turkey. Remove giblets and neck; reserve for other uses. If necessary, remove and discard plastic leg holder and pop-up timer. Rinse well with cold water; drain cavity. Dry turkey well with paper towels. Combine orange zest, garlic, and red pepper; sprinkle over onion slices. Slip your fingers between skin and meat to loosen skin over breast area. Lift skin and carefully tuck onion slices under the skin. Pull the neck skin to the back and twist wing tips to the back, holding the skin in place. Tuck the legs under the band of skin or tie legs to tail with cotton string.

3 Place turkey, breast side up, in basket. Slowly lower basket into hot oil; be cautious of splattering oil. Maintain oil temperature around 350°F. Fry turkey for 3½ minutes per pound. Remove from hot oil to check doneness. Insert an instant read thermometer into the meaty part of the thigh; it is done when it reads 180°F. Remove from hot oil and drain on a wire rack. Let rest 15 minutes.

4 For Orange-Cranberry Sauce, heat butter in a medium saucepan until melted. Stir in garlic, curry powder, and red pepper. Cook 2 minutes. Add 1 cup chicken broth, orange juice concentrate, and cranberries. Increase heat to medium high; bring to a boil. Cook 5 to 7 minutes until syrup-like consistency. Stir cornstarch into remaining ¼ cup chicken broth. Stir cornstarch mixture into sauce; boil 1 minute.

5 Meanwhile, carve turkey; season with salt and pepper. Serve turkey with sauce.

Serves 8 to 10.

Hoisin-Glazed Turkey & Crispy Rice Sticks

Ingredients

Oil

4 fresh or frozen turkey drumsticks (about 3½ pounds)

¾ cup hoisin sauce

⅓ cup honey

⅓ cup rice vinegar

1 tablespoon grated fresh ginger

1 tablespoon minced garlic

1 tablespoon dark sesame oil

3 to 4 tablespoons chopped fresh cilantro

1 tablespoon toasted sesame seeds

Crispy Rice Sticks (recipe below)

Crispy Rice Sticks: Heat peanut oil to 350°F. Carefully pull apart nested rice sticks; use 1½ ounces for topping or 3 ounces to place the turkey legs on top of a bed of crispy rice sticks. Fry rice sticks until puffed, about 30 seconds, turning once. Drain on rack.

COOKING INSTRUCTIONS

1 Preheat oil to 350°F.

2 Completely thaw turkey legs, if frozen. Rinse with cold water; dry well with paper towels. Place turkey legs in basket. Slowly lower basket into hot oil; be cautious of splattering oil. Maintain oil temperature around 350°F. Fry turkey legs for 9 minutes per pound.

3 Meanwhile, combine hoisin sauce, honey, vinegar, ginger, garlic, and sesame oil in a small saucepan, stirring until blended. Cook over medium-low heat 7 to 10 minutes to blend flavors, stirring occasionally.

4 Remove turkey from hot oil to check doneness. Insert an instant-read thermometer into the meaty part of leg; it is done when it reads 180°F. Remove from hot oil and drain on a wire rack. Spoon hoisin glaze over turkey legs. Top with chopped cilantro, sesame seeds, and fried rice sticks.

Serves 8.

Hot Legs

Ingredients

Oil
4 fresh or frozen turkey
  drumsticks (about
  3½ pounds)
¼ cup butter, melted
¼ cup hot pepper sauce
½ cup chunky blue cheese
  dressing
¼ cup chopped celery leaves

COOKING INSTRUCTIONS

If you like hot wings, you'll love this hot leg recipe. I've seen versions of this recipe being sold at festivals and fairs across the south. Must be getting popular!

1 Preheat oil to 350°F.

2 Completely thaw turkey legs, if frozen. Rinse with cold water; dry well with paper towels. Place turkey legs in basket. Slowly lower basket into hot oil; be cautious of splattering oil. Maintain oil temperature around 350°F. Fry turkey legs for 9 minutes per pound.

3 Meanwhile, combine butter and hot pepper sauce in a small bowl.

4 Remove turkey from hot oil to check doneness. Insert an instant read thermometer into the meaty part of leg; it is done when it reads 180°F. Remove from hot oil and drain on a wire rack. Place turkey legs on serving platter; drizzle with hot pepper sauce mixture. Drizzle with some of the dressing and sprinkle with celery leaves. Pass remaining dressing.

Serves 8.

Chapter 4
The Other FRYed Meat

Whole Fried Pork Tenderloin

Ingredients

- Oil
- 2 1- to 1½-pound pork tenderloins
- Chef Williams Cajun Butter Recipe
- Chef Williams Original Cajun Seasoning

COOKING INSTRUCTIONS

In the South, serving sweet potatoes with pork is as important as serving gravy over rice. I recommend baked sweet potatoes as a side, or, if you want something really special, you can email me at reece@chefwilliams.com, and i'll send my wife's Pecan Praline Sweet Potato Casserole recipe—but don't tell her!

1 Preheat oil to 350°F.

2 Wrap pork tenderloin with plastic wrap. Inject with 1½ to 2 ounces of marinade per pound of meat. Remove plastic wrap.

3 Rub outside with Chef Williams Original Cajun Seasoning.

4 Fry 1 pork tenderloin at a time for 12 to 15 minutes or until golden. Remove pork from oil to check doneness. Insert an instant-read thermometer into the thickest portion; it is done when it reads 160°. Remove from hot oil and drain on paper towels.

Serves 8.

Roasted Garlic Pork Tenderloin

Ingredients

Oil

2 1- to 1½-pound pork
     tenderloins

Chef Williams Roasted Garlic
     Recipe

1 5½-ounce package Italian-style
     croutons

2 large eggs

1 cup milk

COOKING INSTRUCTIONS

1 Preheat oil to 350°F.

2 Wrap pork tenderloin with plastic wrap. Inject with 1½ to 2 ounces of marinade per pound of meat. Remove plastic wrap.

3 Process croutons in a food processor until finely ground or place in a heavy-duty plastic bag; squeeze air out and crush with meat mallet or rolling pin. Combine eggs and milk; beat well with a whisk. Dip each tenderloin in egg mixture. Roll in crushed croutons, coating well on all sides.

4 Fry 1 pork tenderloin at a time for 12 to 15 minutes or until golden. Remove pork from oil to check doneness. Insert an instant-read thermometer into the thickest portion; it is done when it reads 160°F. Remove from hot oil and drain on paper towels.

Serves 8.

The Other FRYed Meat

Stuffed Fried Pork Loin

Ingredients

- ¼ cup butter
- 1 cup finely chopped onion
- ½ cup finely chopped sweet pepper
- ½ cup finely chopped celery
- 1 cup sliced fresh mushrooms
- ¾ cup cooked and crumbled bacon
- 1 pound cooked shrimp or crawfish, coarsely chopped
- 2 cups bread crumbs
- 3 tablespoons chopped fresh parsley
  Chef Williams Original Cajun Seasoning
- 1 tablespoon hot sauce
- ½ to 1 cup chicken broth
- 2 3- to 4 pound boneless pork loin roasts
- ¼ cup Chef Williams Cajun Butter Recipe
  Wooden toothpicks
  Oil

COOKING INSTRUCTIONS

1 Melt butter in a large saucepan over medium-high heat. Add onions and sauté 5 minutes or until translucent. Add sweet pepper and celery; cook 8 minutes, stirring constantly. Add mushrooms and bacon; cook for 5 minutes, stirring constantly. Add shrimp, bread crumbs, parsley, 1 tablespoon Chef Williams Original Cajun Seasoning, and hot sauce. Stir in just enough broth to moisten; cook 3 minutes, stirring constantly. Cool completely.

2 Butterfly roasts by making a lengthwise cut down center to, but not through, bottom. Open roasts; lay each flat between 2 pieces of heavy-duty plastic wrap. Using a meat mallet or rolling pin, pound the roasts flat to ½-inch thickness. Spread 2 tablespoons marinade over each roast; lightly sprinkle with additional Chef Williams Original Cajun Seasoning.

3 Spread one-half of the stuffing over each roast leaving a 1-inch border. Starting from a long side, roll up into a spiral, tucking in ends. Secure roasts with long wooden toothpicks or by tying with heavy butcher string at 1-inch intervals. Close all openings with wooden picks (stuffing should not be exposed). Sprinkle with additional Chef Williams Original Cajun Seasoning. Cover and chill at least 30 minutes.

4 Preheat oil to 350°F.

5 Fry 1 roast at a time for 25 to 35 minutes. Remove roast from hot oil and insert an instant-read thermometer in the meat. It is done when it registers 160°F. Remove from hot oil and drain on paper towels. Cover roast completely with a sheet of aluminum foil; let stand 10 minutes. Remove wooden toothpicks or string; carefully slice with a sharp knife. Repeat with remaining roast, if desired, or freeze roast for later use (be sure to thaw completely before frying).

Each roast serves 8 to 10.

Spinach Stuffed Pork Loin

Ingredients

1 pound ground pork sausage

2 cups finely chopped green onions

1 cup finely chopped onion

½ cup finely chopped sweet pepper

½ cup minced fresh parsley

1 tablespoon minced garlic

1 10-ounce package frozen chopped spinach, thawed and drained

2 cups cooked rice

Chef Williams Original Cajun Seasoning

2 4- to 5-pound boneless pork loin roasts

¼ cup Chef Williams Cajun Butter Recipe

Wooden toothpicks

Oil

Sweet Potato Relish (see page 141)

The stuffing makes enough for 2 roasts, which is perfect for a dinner party. If you prefer, you can fry one and wrap one well and freeze for later. The Sweet Potato Relish is a nice finishing touch to this Cajun-style pork delight.

COOKING INSTRUCTIONS

1 Cook ground sausage in a large skillet over medium heat for 12 to 15 minutes or until sausage is brown, stirring until it crumbles. Stir in green onions, onion, sweet pepper, parsley, and garlic; cook 5 minutes, stirring constantly. Stir in spinach, rice, and 2 teaspoons Chef Williams Original Cajun Seasoning; cook for 3 minutes, stirring constantly. Cool completely.

2 Butterfly roasts by making a lengthwise cut down center to, but not through, bottom. Open roast; lay flat between 2 pieces of heavy-duty plastic wrap. Using a meat mallet or rolling pin, pound the roast flat to ½-inch thickness. Spread 2 tablespoons marinade over each roast; lightly sprinkle with Chef Williams Original Cajun Seasoning.

3 Spread one-half sausage mixture over each roast, leaving a 1-inch border. Starting from a long side, roll up into a spiral, tucking in ends. Secure roast with long wooden toothpicks or by tying with heavy butcher string at 1-inch intervals. Close all openings with wooden toothpicks (stuffing should not be exposed). Sprinkle with Chef Williams Original Cajun Seasoning. Cover and chill at least 30 minutes.

4 Preheat oil to 350°F.

5 Fry 1 roast at a time for 25 to 35 minutes. Remove roast from hot oil and insert an instant-read thermometer in the meat. It is done when it registers 160°F. Remove from hot oil and drain on paper towels. Immediately cover roast completely with a sheet of aluminum foil; let stand 10 minutes. Remove wooden toothpicks or string; carefully slice with a sharp knife. Repeat with remaining roast, if desired, or freeze roast for later use (be sure to thaw completely before frying). Serve with Sweet Potato Relish.

Each roast serves 8 to 10.

The Other FRYed Meat

Stuffed Pork Chops

Ingredients

Oil

8 8-ounce bone-in pork chops, 1 inch thick

1 cup Chef Williams Cajun Butter Recipe

1 pound Italian sausage

1 cup finely chopped onion

1 cup Italian-seasoned bread crumbs

Wooden toothpicks

3 cups flour

1 cup cornstarch

2 tablespoons Chef Williams Original Cajun Seasoning

1 tablespoon garlic salt

2 eggs

1½ cups milk

COOKING INSTRUCTIONS

1 Preheat oil to 350°F.

2 Wrap each pork chop with plastic wrap. Inject each pork chop with 1 ounce of marinade; let stand 10 minutes. Remove plastic wrap.

3 Carefully make a 1½-inch incision into side of chop, opposite of bone, with a paring or steak knife. Slice into, but not through chop, creating a nice size pocket.

4 Remove casing from sausage; discard casing. Combine sausage, onion, and bread crumbs; mix well. Stuff each chop with stuffing. Secure pocket opening with a wooden toothpick.

After securing the toothpicks, handle the pork chops gently to avoid knocking the toothpicks out of position. You may use a fully cooked smoked sausage if you prefer.

5 Combine flour, cornstarch, Chef Williams Original Cajun Seasoning, and garlic salt; stir well with a whisk. In another bowl combine eggs and milk; stir well with a whisk. Dredge each chop in seasoned flour. Dip into egg mixture. Dredge again in seasoned flour.

6 Fry 2 chops at a time for 10 to 12 minutes or until sausage stuffing is fully cooked. Remove from hot oil and drain on paper towels.

Serves 8.

Ingredients

- Oil
- 3 pounds beef tenderloin
- 10 ounces Chef Williams Cajun Butter Recipe
- 2 cups all-purpose flour
- 1 tablespoon Chef Williams Original Cajun Seasoning
- 1 teaspoon garlic salt
- 2 large eggs
- 1½ cups milk
- Wooden toothpicks
- Sauce Maurice (see page 153)

COOKING INSTRUCTIONS

1 Preheat oil to 350°F.

2 Cut beef tenderloin into 1-inch pieces; place in a heavy-duty plastic bag. Pour marinade over meat; squeeze air out and seal. Refrigerate 1 hour.

3 Drain beef; discard marinade.

4 Combine flour, Chef Williams Original Cajun Seasoning, and garlic salt; stir well with a whisk. In another bowl combine eggs and milk. Dredge tenderloin in seasoned flour. Dip in egg mixture. Dredge again in seasoned flour.

5 Fry 4 or 5 pieces at a time for 2 to 3 minutes or until golden. Remove from hot oil and drain on paper towels. Pierce each Tid-Bit with a wooden toothpick. Serve warm with Sauce Maurice.

Serves 10 to 12.

The Other FRYed Meat

Ingredients

Oil

1 4- to 6 -pound boneless beef
     prime rib roast

Chef Williams Cajun Butter
     Recipe

Chef Williams Original Cajun
     Seasoning

Sweet Creole Mustard Cream
     (see page 134)

*Ask your neighborhood butcher to
trim and tie the roast to ensure
proper cooking.*

COOKING INSTRUCTIONS

This recipe was my first attempt at deep-frying a large boneless piece of meat. When I removed the roast from the oil, it appeared to be burned. After slicing into the roast, it became evident that the outside (maybe one-eighth of an inch) was the only part that was blackened. The inside was a beautiful, juicy medium rare. We may want to call this a "Deep Fried Blackened Prime Rib."

1 Preheat oil to 350°F.

2 Wrap beef roast with plastic wrap. Inject with 1½ to 2 ounces of marinade per pound of meat. Remove plastic wrap. Pat surface of roast dry with paper towels. Sprinkle with Chef Williams Original Cajun Seasoning.

3 Fry roast 45 minutes to 1 hour (usually about 10 minutes per pound). Remove roast from hot oil to check for doneness. It is done when an instant-read thermometer reads 160°F. (medium doneness). Remove from the oil and drain on paper towels.

4 Cover with a piece of aluminum foil; let stand 10 minutes to rest and to allow the internal temperature to equalize. Carefully carve roast with a sharp slicing knife. Serve with Sweet Creole Mustard Cream.

Serves 8 to 12.

Country Fried Sirloin

Ingredients

Oil
1   2- to 3-pound top sirloin roast
3   cups whole wheat flour
1   tablespoon Chef Williams
     Original Cajun Seasoning
1   teaspoon garlic salt
1   teaspoon black pepper
2   large eggs
1½ cups buttermilk

COOKING INSTRUCTIONS

1   Preheat oil to 350°F.

2   Trim roast, discarding excess fat. Thinly cut meat across the grain into 1-inch-thick cutlets. Place each beef cutlet between 2 sheets of plastic wrap. Pound cutlet to ½-inch thickness using a meat mallet or rolling pin.

3   Combine wheat flour, Chef Williams Original Cajun Seasoning, garlic salt, and pepper; stir well with a whisk. In another bowl combine eggs and buttermilk; beat well with a whisk. Dredge each cutlet in seasoned flour; shake off excess. Dip into egg mixture. Dredge again in seasoned flour, coating all sides completely.

4   Fry 2 or 3 cutlets at a time for 7 to 9 minutes or until golden. Remove from hot oil and drain on paper towels.

Serves 10 to 12.

SERVE WITH:
- *Deep Fried Mashed Potatoes*
  (see page 123)
- *Onion Rings*
  (see page 129)
- *Green Beans and Fried Onions*
  (see page 117)
- *Cajun Cream Gravy*
  (see page 154)

The Other FRYed Meat

Fried Pies with Two Fillings

Ingredients

1 recipe Meat Filling (below) or
   Shrimp and Green Onion
   Filling (see page 67)
2 8-ounce cans refrigerated
   crescent roll dough
   Oil

Meat Filling

1 pound lean ground beef
1 cup finely chopped onion
½ cup finely chopped green sweet
   pepper
1 tablespoon minced garlic
2 tablespoons all-purpose flour
1 teaspoon Chef Williams
   Original Cajun Seasoning
1 teaspoon hot sauce

COOKING INSTRUCTIONS

1 Prepare Meat or Shrimp Filling. For Meat Filling, cook ground beef, onion, sweet pepper, and garlic in hot oil over medium heat for 12 to 15 minutes or until beef is brown, stirring until it crumbles. Stir in flour, Chef Williams Original Cajun Seasoning, and hot sauce; cook 5 minutes, stirring constantly. Cool completely.

2 Unroll cold dough onto a lightly floured surface, working with only 1 can at a time. Separate each piece into 2 rectangles along perforations; cut each piece in half (this will give you eight 4-inch squares per roll). Seal perforations on both sides using fingers.

3 Place 1 tablespoon Meat or Shrimp Filling onto half of each dough square. Moisten edges with just a little water; fold dough over filling. Press edges to seal, then crimp edges with a fork. Repeat procedure with remaining dough and filling. Freeze pies for 10 minutes.

4 Preheat oil to 350°F.

5 Fry 3 or 4 pies at a time for 3 to 4 minutes or until golden, turning once. Remove from hot oil and drain on paper towels. Serve warm.

Makes 16 meat- or shrimp-filled pies.

Shrimp and Green Onion Filling

Ingredients

1 pound fresh or frozen small
    shrimp (36 to 45 per
    pound)
¼ cup butter
2 cups chopped green onions
2 tablespoons all-purpose flour
1 cup half-and-half
1 teaspoon Chef Williams
    Original Cajun Seasoning
½ cup chopped fresh parsley

COOKING INSTRUCTIONS

1 Thaw shrimp if frozen. Peel shrimp, leaving tails on. Using a paring knife, devein shrimp by carefully slicing into meat, but not through, lengthwise down the center of the back. Remove the vein with the tip of a paring knife. Rinse shrimp; pat dry with paper towels.

2 Melt butter in a skillet over medium heat. Add green onions and cook and stir 3 minutes. Stir in flour; cook 1 minute, stirring constantly. Slowly add half-and-half while stirring; stir until smooth. Bring to a simmer; cook 3 to 4 minutes or until thickened, stirring constantly. Stir in shrimp; cook 2 minutes or until shrimp turn pink. Add Chef Williams Original Cajun Seasoning and parsley; stir well. Cool completely.

3 Fill and fry pies as directed beginning with Step 3 on page 66.

Makes filling for 16 pies.

The Other FRYed Meat

Ingredients

- 1 teaspoon salt
- 1 teaspoon black pepper
- 1 teaspoon garlic powder
- 8 4-ounce veal cutlets, thinly sliced
- 8 thin slices ham cut into 4-inch squares
- 8 thin slices Swiss cheese cut into 4-inch squares
  Oil
- 2 cups all-purpose flour
- 1 tablespoon Chef Williams Original Cajun Seasoning
- 2 large eggs
- 1 cup buttermilk

Chicken or pork tenderloin can be substituted for veal, if preferred.

COOKING INSTRUCTIONS

1 Combine salt, pepper, and garlic powder. Set aside.

2 Place each cutlet between 2 sheets of plastic wrap. Pound to a ¼-inch thickness using a meat mallet or rolling pin (the cutlet should be about 6 inches wide). Sprinkle each piece lightly with salt mixture. Place ham and cheese slices onto half of cutlet. Fold other half over ham and cheese, leaving a 1-inch border around slices. Place each cutlet again between 2 sheets of plastic wrap. Gently pound around edges to seal. Chill 30 minutes.

3 Preheat oil to 350°F.

4 Combine flour and Chef Williams Original Cajun Seasoning; stir well with a whisk. In another bowl combine eggs and buttermilk; stir well with a whisk. Dredge each cutlet in seasoned flour. Dip into egg mixture. Dredge again in seasoned flour, coating well.

5 Fry 2 or 3 cutlets at a time for 3 or 4 minutes or until golden. Remove from hot oil and drain on paper towels.

Serves 8.

Whole Fried Chicken

Ingredients

Oil
1 3- to 3½-pound whole fryer
    chicken
   Chef Williams Cajun Butter
    Recipe
   Chef Williams Original Cajun
    Seasoning

Whole fried chicken is prepared basically the same way as whole fried turkey, except it cooks longer per pound of meat. The reason is that chicken has a smaller cavity, so it has less cooking surface exposed to the hot oil.

COOKING INSTRUCTIONS

1 Preheat oil to 350°F.

2 Remove giblets and neck; reserve for other uses. Rinse well with cold water; drain cavity. Dry well with paper towels.

3 Inject ½ cup marinade into each side of breast. Inject ¼ cup marinade into each leg and thigh. Tie legs together with heavy butcher string. Sprinkle with Chef Williams Original Cajun Seasoning.

4 Fry chicken 8 minutes per pound. Remove chicken from hot oil to check for doneness. Insert an instant-read thermometer in the meaty part of the thigh; it is done when it reads 180°F. Remove from hot oil and drain on paper towels.

Serves 4 to 6.

The Other FRYed Meat

Fried Cornish Hens

Ingredients

Oil
8 1¼-pound Cornish game hens
1 cup Chef Williams Cajun
     Butter Recipe
  Chef Williams Original Cajun
     Seasoning

COOKING INSTRUCTIONS

1 Preheat oil to 350°F.

2 Remove giblets from game hens; discard. Rinse hens thoroughly with cold water; pat dry with paper towels. Inject marinade into breast, legs, and thighs. Sprinkle with Chef Williams Original Cajun Seasoning.

3 Fry 2 or 3 hens at a time for 15 minutes. Remove from hot oil and drain on paper towels.

Serves 8.

Ingredients

Oil
8 pounds assorted chicken pieces
6 cups all-purpose flour
¼ cup Chef Williams Original
   Cajun Seasoning
2 large eggs
1 cup milk
⅓ cup Chef Williams Cajun
   Butter Recipe

COOKING INSTRUCTIONS

1 Preheat oil to 350°F.

2 Skin chicken, if desired. Rinse thoroughly with cold water; pat dry with paper towels. Set aside.

3 Combine flour and Chef Williams Original Cajun Seasoning in a bowl; stir well with a whisk. In another bowl beat eggs with a whisk until frothy. Add milk and marinade; stir well with a whisk.

4 Dredge chicken in seasoned flour; shake off excess flour. Dip chicken into egg mixture, allowing excess to drain. Dredge again in seasoned flour.

5 Fry 4 or 5 pieces at a time for 12 to 15 minutes or until golden and chicken is no longer pink near the bone. Remove from hot oil and drain on paper towels.

Serves 12.

The Other FRYed Meat

Parmesan Crusted Chicken Tenders

Ingredients

Oil
4 pounds chicken tenderloins
Chef Williams Original Cajun Seasoning
1½ cups grated Parmesan cheese
1½ cups Italian-seasoned bread crumbs
2 cups all-purpose flour
3 large eggs
½ cup milk

COOKING INSTRUCTIONS

1 Preheat oil to 350°F.

2 Lightly sprinkle chicken tenderloins with Chef Williams Original Cajun Seasoning. Combine Parmesan cheese and bread crumbs; stir well with a whisk. In another bowl combine flour and 2 tablespoons Chef Williams Original Cajun Seasoning. In another bowl combine eggs and milk; stir well with a whisk.

3 Dredge tenderloins in seasoned flour; shake off excess flour.

4 Dip in egg mixture, then roll in Parmesan mixture, coating all sides well.

5 Fry 4 or 5 tenderloins at a time for 4 to 5 minutes or until golden. Remove from hot oil and drain on paper towels.

Serves 10 to 12.

Chicken on a Stick

Ingredients

1 22-ounce jar bread-and-butter pickle slices
6 6-ounce skinnless, boneless chicken breasts
Oil
1 cup all-purpose flour
¾ cup cornstarch
1½ teaspoons salt
1 teaspoon black pepper
1 teaspoon sugar
2 large eggs
1 cup milk
4 medium potatoes, cut into ½-inch slices
2 medium onions, quartered and separated
6 12-inch wooden skewers

A South Carolina favorite! Chicken on a stick is a favorite at festivals and fairs. We've included a little secret: marinate the chicken in bread-and-butter pickle juice. The juice gives the chicken an incredible sweet and tangy flavor.

COOKING INSTRUCTIONS

1 Drain pickles; reserve juice and set pickles aside.

2 Cut chicken into 1-inch pieces. Combine chicken and pickle juice in a heavy-duty plastic bag; seal and refrigerate overnight.

3 Preheat oil to 325°F.

4 Combine flour, cornstarch, salt, pepper, and sugar; stir well with a whisk. Spoon flour mixture onto a small platter or pan. Combine eggs and milk; stir well with a whisk.

5 Drain chicken well; discard pickle juice. Thread potato, onion, pickle, chicken, pickle, onion, and potato onto skewers; repeat until skewers are full. Dip skewers in egg mixture. Dredge in seasoned flour; repeat breading procedure.

6 Fry 4 skewers at a time for 8 to 9 minutes or until golden. Remove from hot oil and drain on paper towels.

Serves 6.

The Other FRYed Meat

Chicken Kiev

Ingredients

- 2 sticks (1 cup) butter
- 2 teaspoons minced garlic
- 2 teaspoons Dijon-style mustard
- 1 teaspoon hot sauce
- 2 tablespoons Chef Williams Original Cajun Seasoning
- 2 tablespoons chopped fresh parsley
- 1 tablespoon minced fresh chives
- 1 teaspoon dried tarragon, crushed (optional)
- Oil
- 8 6-ounce skinless, boneless chicken breasts
- Wooden toothpicks
- 2 cups fine dry bread crumbs
- 4 large eggs
- 1½ cups milk
- 1½ cups all-purpose flour

COOKING INSTRUCTIONS

1 Let sticks of butter stand at room temperature until softened but not melted (do not microwave). Combine soft butter, garlic, mustard, and hot sauce; stir well. Stir in 1 tablespoon Chef Williams Original Cajun Seasoning, parsley, chives, and tarragon, if desired. Mold butter into a log with your fingers on waxed paper. Freeze butter for 1 hour.

2 Preheat oil to 350°F.

3 Place each breast between 2 sheets of plastic wrap. Pound to ¼-inch thickness using a meat mallet or rolling pin. Place 2 tablespoons very cold butter mixture on center of each breast; cover butter with long sides of chicken. Fold each end over and secure with wooden toothpick. Be sure that butter is completely covered.

4 Combine bread crumbs and 2 tablespoons of Chef Williams Original Cajun Seasoning; stir well with a whisk. In another bowl combine eggs and milk; beat well with a whisk. Dredge each chicken piece in flour; shake off excess. Dip into egg mixture. Roll in bread crumbs, coating all sides.

5 Fry 2 or 3 chicken rolls at a time for 7 to 9 minutes or until golden. Remove from hot oil and drain on paper towels.

Serves 8.

Chicken Florentine

Ingredients

- 1 10-ounce package frozen spinach, thawed
- 2 tablespoons olive oil
- ¾ cup finely chopped onion
- 1 4-ounce package crumbled feta cheese
- ¼ cup softened cream cheese
- 2 teaspoons hot sauce
- 1 teaspoon salt
- 8 6-ounce skinless, boneless chicken breasts
- Chef Williams Original Cajun Seasoning
- Wooden toothpicks
- Oil
- 2 cups all-purpose flour
- ¾ cup cornstarch
- 2 teaspoons onion powder
- 1 teaspoon black pepper
- 2 large eggs
- 1½ cups milk

COOKING INSTRUCTIONS

1 Squeeze excess moisture from spinach; place between paper towels and press to remove as much moisture as possible.

2 Heat olive oil in a small skillet over medium heat. Add onion; cook and stir 4 minutes. Add spinach; cook 1 minute, stirring well. Remove from heat; cool 10 minutes. Add feta, cream cheese, hot sauce, and salt; mix well.

3 Place each breast between 2 sheets of plastic wrap. Pound to ¼-inch thickness using a meat mallet or rolling pin. Sprinkle lightly with Chef Williams Original Cajun Seasoning. Place 2 tablespoons filling on center of each breast; cover filling with long sides of chicken; fold each end over and secure with toothpick. Be sure that filling is completely covered and sealed within breast.

4 Preheat oil to 350°F.

5 Combine additional 1 tablespoon Chef Williams Original Cajun Seasoning, flour, cornstarch, onion powder, and black pepper; stir well with a whisk. In another bowl combine eggs and milk; beat well with a whisk. Dredge each chicken breast in seasoned flour; shake off excess. Dip into egg mixture. Dredge again in flour, coating well.

6 Fry 2 or 3 chicken rolls at a time for 7 to 9 minutes or until golden. Remove from hot oil and drain on paper towels. Serve immediately.

Serves 8.

The Other FRYed Meat

Ingredients

2   16-ounce loaves fresh French
      bread, sliced in half
      horizontally
     Mayonnaise
     Creole mustard
3   pounds fried meat of choice
2   cups shredded cabbage
1   ripe tomato, thinly sliced
24 bread-and-butter pickle slices
     Double-Fried French Fries (see
        page 124)
     Creamy Coleslaw (see
        page 131)

COOKING INSTRUCTIONS

1 Toast bread, if desired. Spread cut sides of each loaf with desired amount of mayonnaise and mustard. Layer with meat of your choice, shredded cabbage, tomato, and pickles.

2 Cut each sandwich into quarters.

3 Serve sandwiches with Double-Fried French Fries and Creamy Coleslaw.

Serves 8.

Peanut Butter and Banana Sandwich

Ingredients

Oil
½ cup creamy or crunchy peanut butter
8 slices white bread
1 ripe, but firm, banana
2¼ cups packaged biscuit mix
1¼ cups water
Powdered sugar

It is said this was one of Elvis Presley's favorite meals.

COOKING INSTRUCTIONS

Not only was this one of Elvis Presley's favorite meals, but the host at almost every television show I have cooked for claimed this to be a favorite as well.

1 Preheat oil to 350°F.

2 Spread 2 tablespoons of peanut butter on each of 4 slices of bread. Cut banana into 4 equal parts, then slice the parts 3 times. Put 3 slices each on 4 slices of bread. Bring bread together to form 4 peanut butter and banana sandwiches. Combine biscuit mix and water; stir well with a whisk. Dip sandwiches in batter, coating all sides well.

3 Fry 1 sandwich at a time for 30 seconds while pushing sandwich into hot oil with tongs or a large utensil. Let sandwich float to top; fry 2 minutes, turning once. Remove from hot oil and drain on paper towels. Sprinkle lightly with powdered sugar.

Serves 4.

The Other FRYed Meat

Black Bean Burgers

Ingredients

3 19-ounce cans black beans,
    rinsed and drained
1 cup minced onion
1 tablespoon minced garlic
½ cup chunky salsa
1 large egg
2 large egg yolks
1½ teaspoons ground cumin
1 teaspoon Chef Williams
    Original Cajun Seasoning
2 cups bread crumbs
   Oil
   Hamburger buns
   Chunky salsa
   Sour cream

COOKING INSTRUCTIONS

1 In a large bowl mash beans using the back of a large spoon. Add onion, garlic, salsa, egg, egg yolks, cumin, and 1 teaspoon Chef Williams Original Cajun Seasoning; mix well.

2 Stir in 1 cup bread crumbs. Using wet hands, shape into 8 patties. Roll in remaining cup of bread crumbs, coating all sides well. Cover and chill 1 hour.

3 Preheat oil to 350°F.

4 Fry patties in 2 batches for 3 to 4 minutes or until golden. Remove from hot oil and drain on paper towels. Serve warm on a hamburger bun with salsa and sour cream.

Serves 8.

Incredible Corn Dogs

Ingredients

Oil
1½ cups cornmeal
1 cup all-purpose flour
½ cup sugar
2 teaspoons baking powder
1½ teaspoons salt
¾ teaspoon black pepper
2 large eggs
¼ cup Chef Williams Cajun
Butter Recipe
¾ cup half-and-half
2 12-ounce packages hot dogs
(regular size)
16 10-inch wooden skewers
Creole mustard

COOKING INSTRUCTIONS

1 Preheat oil to 375°F.

2 Combine cornmeal, flour, sugar, baking powder, salt, and pepper; stir well with a whisk. In another bowl combine eggs, marinade, and half-and-half; stir well. Combine cornmeal mixture and egg mixture; mix until dry ingredients are moistened.

3 Pat hot dogs dry with paper towels. Secure hot dogs onto wooden skewers. Dip into batter, coating all sides well.

4 Fry a few hot dogs at a tIme for 3 minutes or until golden. Remove from hot oil and drain on paper towels. Serve warm with Creole mustard.

Serves 16.

The Other FRYed Meat

Chapter 5
Wild FRYeds

Ingredients

Oil
8 4-ounce venison cutlets
2 cups buttermilk
4 ounces Chef Williams Cajun
    Butter Recipe
1½ cups all-purpose flour
1½ cups cornstarch
2 tablespoons Chef Williams
    Original Cajun Seasoning
2 teaspoons garlic powder
1 teaspoon dry mustard
2 large eggs
2 cups buttermilk
Cajun Cream Gravy (see
    page 154)

COOKING INSTRUCTIONS

One great thing about injecting marinade into venison is that the marinade pretty much eliminates the wild flavor. An option to consider when marinating venison is to add melted butter to the marinade. Venison, unlike beef, has no fat marbled through the meat. The melted butter will help the venison with juiciness and flavor.

1 Preheat oil to 350°F.

2 Place each cutlet between 2 sheets of plastic wrap. Pound to ¼-inch thickness using a meat mallet or rolling pin; place in a large heavy-duty plastic bag. Combine 2 cups buttermilk and marinade; stir well. Pour buttermilk mixture over venison; squeeze air out of bag and seal. Refrigerate overnight.

3 Drain venison; discard liquid. Combine flour, cornstarch, Chef Williams Original Cajun Seasoning, garlic powder, and dry mustard; stir well with a whisk. In another bowl combine eggs and the remaining 2 cups fresh buttermilk; stir with a whisk until smooth. Dredge each piece of venison in seasoned flour; shake off excess. Dip into egg mixture. Dredge again in seasoned flour, coating well.

4 Fry 2 or 3 cutlets at a time for 2 to 3 minutes or until golden. Remove from hot oil and drain on paper towels. Serve warm with Cajun Cream Gravy.

Serves 4.

Venison with Smoked Bacon Shallot Sauce

Ingredients

Oil
1 3- to 4-pound venison loin
   Chef Williams Cajun Garlic
      Recipe
   Chef Williams Original Cajun
      Seasoning
1 teaspoon freshly ground black
      pepper
8 slices bacon
1 cup chopped green onions
1 tablespoon minced garlic
2 tablespoons sherry vinegar
1 cup beef stock

*Injecting the venison loin with
marinade not only keeps the meat
moist but also adds a savory grilled
onion flavor.*

COOKING INSTRUCTIONS

1 Preheat oil to 350°F.

2 Wrap loin with plastic wrap and inject loin with marinade, using 2 ounces per pound. Sprinkle with Chef Williams Original Cajun Seasoning and black pepper.

3 Fry for 7 to 8 minutes per pound or until internal temperature reaches 140°F. Remove from hot oil and cover loosely with foil. Set aside.

4 Cook bacon until crisp; crumble and set aside. Reserve drippings. Add green onions and garlic to drippings and cook and stir until wilted. Add sherry vinegar and cook until reduced by half. Add stock and cook on medium-high heat until thickened. Add crumbled bacon. Slice venison; pour sauce on top.

Serves 8 to 10.

Crispy Cajun-Style Peking Duck

Ingredients

- 1 4- to 5-pound duckling
  Chef Williams Teriyaki Honey
    Recipe
- 1 small orange or tangerine,
    halved
- 4 cloves garlic, smashed
- 1 quart water
  Oil
- ½ cup all-purpose flour
  Chef Williams Original Cajun
    Seasoning

This recipe is a slightly difficult to prepare! The duckling needs 2 hours to dry under a fan. The secret to getting the skin crispy is to remove as much moisture from the skin as possible. The skin will not crisp if too wet. This dish is popular in many Asian restaurants, but many require a 24-hour notice to prepare it in the proper fashion.

COOKING INSTRUCTIONS

1 Trim duckling of excess fat. Rinse well with cold water. Wrap duckling with plastic wrap. Inject with 1½ to 2 ounces of marinade per pound of meat; let stand 10 minutes. Remove plastic wrap. Place orange and garlic in cavity. Tie ends of legs together with heavy string. Place on a roasting rack in a shallow pan; pour water over duckling. Cover pan with aluminum foil. Bake at 250°F for 1½ hours. Remove from oven and let cool 15 minutes.

2 Remove orange and garlic; discard. Place duckling on a food rack; pat dry with paper towels. Position duck in front of a fan set on high and allow to air-dry for 2 hours, making sure the air blows directly onto duck.

3 Preheat oil to 400°F.

4 Dust duck with flour; shake off excess. Fry duck until skin is crispy. Remove from hot oil and drain on paper towels. Sprinkle with Chef Williams Original Cajun Seasoning. Carefully carve with a sharp knife.

Serves 2 to 4.

Blue Cheese-Stuffed Quail in Ale Batter

Ingredients

Oil

1 pound sweet Italian sausage

¼ cup plus 2 tablespoons crumbled Gorgonzola or other blue cheese

1 teaspoon dried sage, crushed

¾ teaspoon salt

½ teaspoon black pepper

8 quail, dressed

Chef Williams Original Cajun Seasoning

Wooden toothpicks

2 cups all-purpose flour

2 teaspoons baking powder

1½ teaspoons salt

1 12-ounce bottle ice cold beer

Sweet Creole Mustard Cream (see page 134)

COOKING INSTRUCTIONS

Deep fried quail was one of our most popular specialties at The Front Porch Restaurant. One of the sides we offered with this recipe was grits and gravy—another southern specialty. Google it!

1 Preheat oil to 350°F.

2 Remove sausage from casing. Brown sausage in a skillet over medium heat, stirring to crumble meat. Remove from heat and cool 10 minutes. Add Gorgonzola, sage, salt, and pepper; mix well.

3 Rinse quail well with cold water; pat dry with paper towels. Sprinkle with Chef Williams Original Cajun Seasoning. Divide stuffing into 8 portions. Stuff each portion into cavity of each quail; secure cavity with wooden toothpicks.

4 Combine flour, baking powder, and salt; stir well with a whisk. Add beer; stir well until smooth. Dip each quail into batter, coating all sides well.

5 Fry 2 or 3 quail at a time for 6 to 8 minutes or until golden, turning several times. Remove from heat and drain on paper towels. Glaze meat with Sweet Creole Mustard Cream.

Serves 8.

Wild FRYeds

Ingredients

- 20 skinless, boneless dove breasts
- 4 cups buttermilk
  Oil
- 1 12-ounce package bacon
  Wooden toothpicks

COOKING INSTRUCTIONS

In the 1990s, I met a great group of people that produced a show called *Michigan Outdoors*. While cooking on this show, I learned to substitute some of their Northern game into my Southern recipes. Pheasant and grouse work really well in this recipe.

1 Place dove breasts in a large heavy-duty plastic bag. Pour buttermilk over meat; squeeze air out and seal. Refrigerate overnight.

2 Preheat oil to 350°F.

3 Drain dove breasts; discard buttermilk. Cut each bacon strip in half. Wrap dove breast with a piece of bacon. Secure with a wooden toothpick.

4 Fry a few breasts at a time for 1½ to 2 minutes or until bacon is crisp. Remove from hot oil and drain on paper towels.

Makes 20 breasts.

Coconut-Crusted Alligator

Ingredients

Oil
2 pounds alligator loin meat
4 cups water, room temperature
2 tablespoons salt
2 cups all-purpose flour
1 tablespoon Chef Williams
    Original Cajun Seasoning
3 large eggs
1/4 cup heavy cream
1 14-ounce package flaked
    coconut

COOKING INSTRUCTIONS

1 Preheat oil to 350°F.

2 Cut alligator into 1½-inch pieces. Combine alligator, water, and salt in a large bowl; stir well. Let stand 15 minutes, stirring twice. Drain well; pat meat dry with paper towels.

3 Combine flour and Chef Williams Original Cajun Seasoning; stir well with a whisk. In another bowl combine eggs and cream; beat well with a whisk. Dredge alligator in seasoned flour. Dip in egg mixture. Roll in flaked coconut, coating well on all sides.

4 Fry 4 or 5 alligator pieces at a time for 2 to 3 minutes or until golden brown. Remove from hot oil and drain on paper towels.

Serves 10 to 12.

Chapter 6
Sea FRYed

Lemon Sole à la Reecé

Ingredients

- 4 whole fresh or frozen lemon sole or winter flounder fillets, dressed
- 1 cup Chef Williams Cajun Garlic Recipe Oil
- 1½ cups all-purpose flour
- 1½ cups cornstarch
- 2 tablespoons Chef Williams Original Cajun Seasoning
- 2 teaspoons garlic powder
- 1 teaspoon dry mustard
- 3 eggs
- 1½ cups buttermilk
- 2 lemons, cut into wedges

Ask to have your fresh fish dressed when visiting your favorite local seafood market.

COOKING INSTRUCTIONS

1 Thaw fish, if frozen. Rinse fish; pat dry with paper towels. Place fish in a large heavy-duty plastic bag; pour marinade over fish. Remove as much air as possible; seal. Chill 1 hour.

2 Preheat oil to 350°F.

3 Combine flour, cornstarch, Chef Williams Original Cajun Seasoning, garlic powder, and dry mustard; stir well with a whisk. In another bowl combine eggs and buttermilk; stir well with a whisk.

4 Remove fish from marinade. Dredge in flour mixture. Dip into egg mixture. Dredge again in flour mixture.

5 Fry 2 fillets at a time for 6 to 10 minutes or until golden. Remove from hot oil and drain on paper towels. Garnish with lemon wedges.

Serves 4.

Grouper Sandwich Topped with Coleslaw

Ingredients

Oil

2½ cups all-purpose flour

1 tablespoon Chef Williams Original Cajun Seasoning

8 4-ounce fresh or frozen grouper fillets lets, square cut

1 cup buttermilk

8 onion-topped sandwich buns, split and toasted

2 cups Creamy Coleslaw (see page 131)

COOKING INSTRUCTIONS

Fried grouper is my favorite sandwich in the whole wide world. A.J.'s Restaurant in Destin, Florida, served me my first grouper sandwich. This is my version:

1 Preheat oil to 350°F.

2 Combine flour and Chef Williams Original Cajun Seasoning in a shallow bowl; stir well.

3 Thaw fish, if frozen. Rinse fish; pat dry with paper towels. Dredge grouper in flour mixture; dip in buttermilk and dredge in flour mixture again.

4 Fry 2 or 3 fillets at a time for 5 to 6 minutes or until golden. Remove from hot oil and drain on paper towels. Place a fillet on the bottom half of each bun. Top with ¼ cup coleslaw. Add bun tops.

Serves 8.

Catfish Maurice

Ingredients

- 2 pounds fresh or frozen crawfish tails
- 4 pounds fresh or frozen catfish fillets, thinly sliced
- 2 cups chopped onions
- ½ cup butter, melted
- 1 cup chopped sweet pepper
- 1 cup chopped celery
- 1 tablespoon minced garlic
- 3 tablespoons all-purpose flour
  Chef Williams Original Cajun Seasoning
- 1 tablespoon tomato paste
- 1 14-ounce can chicken broth
  Oil
- 2 cups cornmeal

COOKING INSTRUCTIONS

Fried catfish topped with crawfish etouffee has become one of the most popular recipes served in Louisiana restaurants. Try it and you'll understand why.

1 Thaw crawfish tails and catfish fillets, if frozen. Rinse tails and fillets; pat dry with paper towels. Set aside.

2 For crawfish etouffée, cook and stir onions in melted butter over medium-high heat for 5 minutes or until tender. Add sweet pepper, celery, and garlic; cook 5 minutes, stirring constantly. Sprinkle with flour and 1 tablespoon Chef Williams Original Cajun Seasoning; stir well. Cook 2 minutes, stirring constantly. Add tomato paste and chicken broth; stir well. Bring to a boil; reduce heat. Simmer, covered, for 12 minutes, stirring occasionally. Stir in crawfish tails. Return to a simmer; cook 2 minutes, stirring constantly.

3 Preheat oil to 350°F.

4 Combine cornmeal and additional 2 tablespoons Chef Williams Original Cajun Seasoning; stir well with a whisk. Evenly coat all sides of catfish with cornmeal mixture. Fry 3 or 4 fillets at a time for 4 to 5 minutes or until golden. Remove from hot oil and drain on paper towels. Serve hot catfish topped with hot crawfish etouffée.

Serves 12.

Crispy Catfish Dinner

Ingredients

Oil

5 pounds fresh or frozen catfish fillets, thinly sliced

1½ cups buttermilk

Chef Williams Original Cajun Seasoning

3 cups self-rising cornmeal

COOKING INSTRUCTIONS

1 Preheat oil to 375°F.

2 Thaw fish, if frozen. Rinse fish; pat dry with paper towels. Dip catfish in buttermilk; allow excess buttermilk to drain off. Sprinkle with Chef Williams Original Cajun Seasoning. Dredge in cornmeal.

3 Fry 3 or 4 fillets at a time for 3 to 4 minutes or until golden brown (fillets will float when done). Remove from hot oil and drain well on paper towels.

Serves 10.

FOR A TRUE CATFISH FRY SERVE WITH:
- *Beer Cheese Hushpuppies (see page 113)*
- *Double-Fried French Fries (see page 124)*
- *Creamy Coleslaw (see page 131)*
- *Baked Beans (see page 130)*
- *Green Onion Tarter Sauce (see page 143)*

Spicy Cajun Catfish Burgers

Ingredients

- 4 6-ounce fresh or frozen catfish fillets
- 1 cup water
- ½ cup Chef Williams Cajun Butter Recipe
- 2 large eggs
- 3 tablespoons mayonnaise
- 2 tablespoons Creole mustard
- 1½ teaspoons Chef Williams Original Cajun Seasoning
- ½ teaspoon dry mustard
- ½ teaspoon garlic salt
- 1 cup finely ground butter cracker crumbs
- Oil
- 1 red onion, thinly sliced
- 1 tomato, thinly sliced
- 6 gourmet hamburger buns, toasted
- Green Onion Tartar Sauce (see page 143)

COOKING INSTRUCTIONS

1 Preheat oven to 450°F.

2 Thaw fish, if frozen. Rinse fish; pat dry with paper towels. Combine water and marinade; pour into a large baking dish. Place catfish in baking dish; cover. Bake at 450° for 10 minutes or until fish flakes when tested with a fork. Drain fish and cool completely.

3 Combine eggs, mayonnaise, Creole mustard, Chef Williams Original Cajun Seasoning, dry mustard, and garlic salt; stir well with a whisk. Flake fish into small pieces using a fork. Gently toss fish with egg mixture. Form mixture into 6 patties. Coat fish burgers with cracker crumbs on all sides. Chill 1 hour.

4 Preheat oil to 375°F.

5 Fry 2 or 3 burgers at a time for 5 to 6 minutes or until golden. Remove from hot oil and drain on paper towels. Serve fish burgers warm, with onion and tomato, on a toasted bun spread with Green Onion Tartar Sauce.

Serves 6.

Sesame-Crusted Catfish

Ingredients

- 4 pounds fresh or frozen catfish fillets, thinly sliced
- ½ cup prepared mustard
  Oil
- 1½ cups cornmeal
- ½ cup sesame seeds
- 3 tablespoons Chef Williams Original Cajun Seasoning

COOKING INSTRUCTIONS

1 Thaw fish, if frozen. Rinse fish; pat dry with paper towels. Cut fish into 2-inch pieces. Combine fish and mustard; chill 15 minutes.

2 Preheat oil to 350°F.

3 Combine cornmeal, sesame seeds, and Chef Williams Original Cajun Seasoning; stir well with a whisk. Evenly coat all sides of catfish with cornmeal mixture.

4 Fry 6 or 8 pieces at a time for 4 to 5 minutes or until golden. Remove from hot oil and drain on paper towels.

Serves 12.

Crispy Battered Shrimp

Ingredients

4 pounds fresh or frozen large
    shrimp (20 to 24 per
    pound)
  Oil
2 cups all-purpose flour
2 tablespoons Chef Williams
    Original Cajun Seasoning
3 cups packaged pancake mix
4 cups seltzer water

COOKING INSTRUCTIONS

1 Thaw shrimp, if frozen. Peel shrimp, leaving tails on. Using a paring knife, devein shrimp by carefully slicing into meat, but not through, lengthwise down the center line of the back. Remove vein with tip of a paring knife. Rinse shrimp; pat dry with a paper towel. Set aside.

2 Preheat oil to 350°F.

3 Combine flour and Chef Williams Original Cajun Seasoning in a bowl; stir well with a whisk. In another bowl combine pancake mix and seltzer water; stir well with a whisk.

4 Dredge shrimp in seasoned flour; shake off excess. Dip shrimp into batter, letting excess batter drain. Dredge again in seasoned flour. Fry 5 or 6 shrimp at a time for 2 to 3 minutes or until golden. Remove from hot oil and drain on paper towels.

Serves 12 to 14.

Deep Fried Stuffed Jumbo Shrimp

Ingredients

- ½ 1-pound loaf French bread
- ½ cup water
- ¼ cup butter
- 2 cups chopped onions
- 1 cup chopped sweet pepper
- 1 cup chopped celery
- 1 tablespoon minced garlic
- 1 1-pound package frozen peeled small shrimp, thawed, rinsed, drained, and coarsely chopped
- 1 pound fresh or frozen crabmeat, picked over
- 4 large eggs
  Chef Williams Original Cajun Seasoning
- 3 pounds fresh or frozen jumbo shrimp (16 to 20 per pound)
- 1½ cups all-purpose flour
  Oil
  Rémoulade Sauce (see page 150)

COOKING INSTRUCTIONS

1 Tear French bread into chunks; drizzle with water and mix well to moisten. Squeeze to remove excess water; break chunks into small pieces using hands. Set aside.

2 Melt butter in a skillet over medium-high heat. Add onions, sweet pepper, celery, and garlic; saute 5 minutes. Add reserved moistened French bread and small shrimp; cook 3 or 4 minutes or until shrimp turn pink. Remove from heat. Cool completely.

3 Thaw crabmeat, if frozen. Rinse crabmeat; pat dry with paper towels. Combine shrimp mixture, crabmeat, eggs, and 1 tablespoon Chef Williams Original Cajun Seasoning; mix well. Cover and chill 1 hour.

4 Thaw jumbo shrimp, if frozen. Peel shrimp, leaving tails on. Using a paring knife, devein shrimp by carefully slicing into meat, but not through, lengthwise down the center line of the back. Remove the vein with the tip of a paring knife. Open the shrimp to lie flat. Rinse shrimp; pat shrimp dry with paper towels. Sprinkle lightly with additional Chef Williams Original Cajun Seasoning.

5 Mold 1 rounded teaspoon of stuffing firmly onto each shrimp. Cover and chill 1 hour. Combine flour and 1 tablespoon Chef Williams Original Cajun Seasoning stir well with a whisk. Dredge shrimp in seasoned flour.

6 Preheat oil to 350°F.

7 Fry 4 or 5 shrimp at a time for 2 to 3 minutes or until golden, turning once. Remove from hot oil and drain on paper towels. Serve warm with Rémoulade Sauce.

Serves 10 to 12.

  97

Sea FRYed

Crab-Stuffed Shrimp

Ingredients

- ¼ cup butter
- 1 medium onion, finely chopped
- 2 celery stalks, finely chopped
- 1 small green sweet pepper, finely chopped
- 1 tablespoon minced garlic
- 1 teaspoon minced jalapeño pepper
- Chef Williams Original Cajun Seasoning
- 1 teaspoon dried basil, crushed
- ¾ teaspoon dried oregano, crushed
- 1 teaspoon hot sauce
- 2 cups fresh or frozen lump crabmeat, picked over
- 1 cup fine dry bread crumbs
- 2 egg yolks
- 2½ pounds jumbo shrimp (16 to 20 per pound)
- Oil
- 3 cups all-purpose flour
- 2 cups milk
- 3 large eggs
- Rémoulade Sauce (see page 150)

COOKING INSTRUCTIONS

1 Melt butter in a skillet over medium-high heat. Add onion; cook and stir 5 minutes or until lightly browned. Add celery, sweet pepper, garlic, and jalapeño; cook and stir 5 minutes. Remove from heat; stir in 1 teaspoon Chef Williams Original Cajun Seasoning, basil, oregano, and hot sauce. Cool completely.

2 Thaw crabmeat, if frozen. Rinse crabmeat; pat dry with paper towels. Combine onion mixture, bread crumbs, crabmeat, and egg yolks; mix well. Cover and chill 1 hour.

3 Thaw shrimp, if frozen. Peel shrimp, leaving tails on. Using a paring knife, devein shrimp by carefully slicing into meat, but not through, lengthwise down the center line of the back. Remove the vein with the tip of a paring knife. Open the shrimp to lie flat. Rinse shrimp; pat dry with paper towels. Sprinkle lightly with additional Chef Williams Original Cajun Seasoning.

4 Preheat oil to 350°F.

5 Combine flour and an additional 2 teaspoons Chef Williams Original Cajun Seasoning; stir well with a whisk. In another bowl combine milk and eggs; stir well with a whisk. Dredge shrimp into seasoned flour. Place 1 tablespoon crab mixture on top of each open shrimp. Mold stuffing firmly onto shrimp.

6 Dredge each stuffed shrimp in seasoned flour; shake off excess. Dip into egg mixture. Dip again into seasoned flour. Fry 4 or 5 shrimp at a time for 2 to 3 minutes or until golden, turning once. Remove from hot oil and drain on paper towels. Serve warm with Rémoulade Sauce.

Serves 8 to 10.

Shrimp in Eggplant Batter

Ingredients

¼ cup butter

1 cup chopped onion

1 tablespoon minced garlic

6 cups peeled and chopped
    eggplant

1 tablespoon brown sugar

   Chef Williams Original Cajun
    Seasoning

¾ teaspoon dried oregano,
    crushed

½ teaspoon dried thyme, crushed

1½ teaspoons salt

¾ cup corn flour (masa harina)

¾ cup all-purpose flour

2 large eggs

¾ cup beer

½ cup cream

4 pounds fresh or frozen large
    shrimp (20 to 24 per
    pound)

   Oil

   Rémoulade Sauce (see
    page 150)

*The battered shrimp need to fry
until reaching a dark golden color.
The eggplant batter acts as an
insulation for the shrimp, so it takes
a little extra frying time to ensure
that the shrimp are fully cooked.*

COOKING INSTRUCTIONS

1 Melt butter in a skillet over medium-high heat. Add onions; cook and stir 5 minutes or until softened. Add garlic; cook and stir 1 minute. Add eggplant; cook 10 minutes, stirring often. Add brown sugar; cook 2 minutes. Remove from heat; cool completely. Process eggplant mixture in a food mill, food processor, or blender until smooth. Stir in 1 teaspoon Chef Williams Original Cajun Seasoning, oregano, thyme, and salt.

2 Combine corn flour and flour; stir well with a whisk. In another bowl, beat eggs well with a whisk. Add eggplant puree, beer, and cream; stir well. Add flour mixture; stir until smooth. Cover and chill 1 hour.

3 Thaw shrimp, if frozen. Peel shrimp leaving tails on. Using a paring knife, devein shrimp by carefully slicing into meat, but not through, lengthwise down center line of the back. Remove vein with tip of a paring knife. Rinse shrimp; pat dry with paper towels. Sprinkle lightly with additional Chef Williams Original Cajun Seasoning.

4 Preheat oil to 350°F.

5 Dip shrimp into eggplant batter several times, coating with a thick layer of batter. Fry 7 or 8 shrimp at a time for 2 to 3 minutes or until golden, turning once. Remove from hot oil and drain on paper towels. Serve with Rémoulade Sauce.

Serves 8.

Grit Cakes with Shrimp Gravy

Ingredients

- 4 cups water
- 2 cups milk
- 2 cups half-and-half
- ¼ cup butter
- 1 tablespoon salt
- 2 cups uncooked regular grits
  Oil
  Shrimp Gravy (see page 101)
- 1 bunch green onions, thinly sliced

COOKING INSTRUCTIONS

1 Combine water, milk, half-and-half, butter, and salt in a large saucepan. Bring to a boil. Stir vigorously with a whisk while slowly pouring grits in a steady stream. Return to a boil. Reduce heat and simmer, covered, 10 to 15 minutes, stirring constantly. When grits are tender, immediately pour into a lightly greased 15×10×1-inch baking sheet; level top with a flat metal spatula. Refrigerate 2 hours.

2 Prepare Shrimp Gravy.

3 Preheat oil to 350°F.

4 Slice grits lengthwise down the center. Slice lengthwise down the center of each half, creating 4 rows lengthwise. Slice crosswise into 5 equal rows to create 15 (3×2-inch) square grit cakes. Slice each grit cake in half diagonally into 2 triangles.

5 Fry a few cakes at a time for 2 to 3 minutes or until golden, turning once. Remove from hot oil and drain on paper towels. Serve warm with Shrimp Gravy; sprinkle with green onions.

6 Extra grit cakes can be wrapped in plastic wrap, placed in a heavy-duty plastic bag, and frozen. Thaw completely before frying.

Makes 15 Grit Cakes.

Shrimp Gravy

Ingredients

- 3 pounds fresh or frozen large shrimp (20 to 24 per pound)
- 4 cups chicken broth
- ¼ cup butter
- ¾ pound salt-cured country ham, finely chopped
- 3 tablespoons minced garlic
- 1 pound fresh mushrooms, sliced
- ¼ cup all-purpose flour
- 2 tablespoons hot sauce
  Grit Cakes (see page 100)

This wonderful gravy takes advantage of salt-cured country ham, which gives the dish a very distinct saltiness.

COOKING INSTRUCTIONS

1 Thaw shrimp, if frozen. Peel shrimp; reserve shells. Using a paring knife, devein shrimp by carefully slicing into meat, but not through, lengthwise down the center line of the back. Remove the vein with the tip of a paring knife. Rinse shrimp; pat dry with paper towels. Set shrimp aside.

2 Combine reserved shrimp shells and chicken broth in a large saucepan. Bring to a boil; reduce heat and simmer, uncovered, 15 minutes. Strain broth through a wire mesh strainer; discard shells. Cool.

3 Melt butter in a skillet over medium-high heat. Add ham and garlic; cook and stir 2 minutes. Add mushrooms; cook 8 minutes, stirring constantly. Sprinkle with flour; cook 2 minutes, stirring constantly. Slowly add broth, 1 cup at a time, stirring after each addition. Bring to a simmer; cook 2 minutes or until mixture is thickened, stirring constantly. Add reserved shrimp and hot sauce; return to a simmer. Cook 3 to 4 minutes or until shrimp turn pink, stirring constantly. Serve hot over Grit Cakes.

Serves 6 to 8.

Cheddar 'n Crawfish Pies

Ingredients

1 cup chopped onion
½ cup chopped green sweet pepper
1 tablespoon minced garlic
¼ cup butter, melted
1 tablespoon all-purpose flour
¼ cup beer
¼ cup milk
1 1-pound package fresh or frozen crawfish tails, peeled and rinsed
1½ teaspoons Chef Williams Original Cajun Seasoning
1 cup grated sharp cheddar cheese
Oil
½ cup all-purpose flour
1 20.8-ounce package frozen cheddar and garlic biscuits or regular biscuits, thawed

The flavored biscuit dough adds a special touch to these simple pies.

COOKING INSTRUCTIONS

1 Cook and stir onion, bell pepper, and garlic in butter for 5 minutes or until tender. Sprinkle with flour; cook 2 minutes, stirring constantly. Add beer and milk; cook 3 to 4 minutes or until well thickened, stirring constantly. Thaw crawfish, if frozen. Add crawfish, 1½ teaspoons Chef Williams Original Cajun Seasoning, and cheese; stir until cheese is melted. Set aside and cool completely.

2 Preheat oil to 375°F.

3 On a clean cutting board or on a marble slab, sprinkle flour and rub into surface. Lightly sprinkle each biscuit with flour. Roll each biscuit into a 6-inch circle. Spoon 1½ tablespoons crawfish filling onto half of each biscuit circle. Moisten edges with just a little water; fold dough over crawfish filling, pressing to seal edges. Crimp edges with a fork.

4 Fry 2 to 3 pies at a time for 4 to 5 minutes or until golden. Remove from hot oil and drain on paper towels. Serve warm.

Serves 12.

Fried Oysters

Ingredients

Oil
3 cups all-purpose flour
1 cup corn flour (masa harina)
2 tablespoons Chef Williams
   Original Cajun Seasoning
2 pints shucked oysters in liquid

COOKING INSTRUCTIONS

1 Preheat oil to 350°F.

2 Combine flour, corn flour, and Chef Williams Original Cajun Seasoning in a bowl; stir well with a whisk. Dip wet oysters in flour mixture, coating well.

3 Fry 8 or 9 oysters at a time for about 2 minutes, turning once. Remove from hot oil and drain on paper towels.

Serves 8.

Sea FRYed

Potato Chip-Crusted Scallops

Ingredients

Oil
1 13-ounce package salted
    potato chips
1 cup fine dry bread crumbs
2 teaspoons Chef Williams
    Original Cajun Seasoning
2 large eggs
½ cup milk
24 fresh or frozen large sea
    scallops (2 pounds)
1 cup all-purpose flour

COOKING INSTRUCTIONS

1 Preheat oil to 350°F.

2 Process potato chips in a food processor until finely ground. Combine ground potato chips, bread crumbs, and 1 teaspoon Chef Williams Original Cajun Seasoning; mix well. In another bowl combine eggs and milk; beat well with a whisk. Set aside.

3 Thaw scallops, if frozen. Rinse scallops; pat dry with paper towels. Sprinkle each scallop evenly with remaining Chef Williams Original Cajun Seasoning. Dredge in flour; shake off excess. Dip scallops into egg mixture; roll in potato chip mixture, coating all sides evenly.

4 Fry 5 or 6 scallops at a time for 3 to 4 minutes (depending on the size of the scallops) or until golden. Remove from hot oil and drain on paper towels. Serve immediately.

Serves 8.

Tempura Lobster

Ingredients

- 4 8- to 10-ounce fresh or frozen lobster tails
- 4 12-inch wooden skewers
- Oil
- 1 cup all-purpose flour
- 1 cup cornstarch
- 1 tablespoon Chef Williams Original Cajun Seasoning
- 1 teaspoon garlic powder
- 1 teaspoon onion powder
- 1 teaspoon black pepper
- 2 cups buttermilk

COOKING INSTRUCTIONS

1 Thaw lobster, if frozen. Remove shell of lobster by cutting shell with kitchen scissors or a knife, leaving tail fan on. Rinse lobster tail meat; pat dry with paper towels. Using a paring knife, devein lobster by carefully slicing 1/4 inch into meat, lengthwise down the center line of its back. Remove the vein with the tip of a paring knife. Rinse again; pat dry with paper towels. Thread lobster tails onto wooden skewers (this keeps the lobster tail straight).

2 Preheat oil to 325°F.

3 Combine flour, cornstarch, Chef Williams Original Cajun Seasoning, garlic powder, onion powder, and pepper; stir well with a whisk.

4 Dredge lobster tail in flour mixture; shake off excess. Dip into buttermilk. Repeat procedure, then dredge one last time in flour mixture.

5 Fry 2 tails at a time for 6 to 8 minutes or until golden (be careful not to overcook). Remove from hot oil and drain on paper towels. Remove skewers and serve immediately.

Serves 4.

Sea FRYed

Calamari Caesar

Ingredients

Oil

3 large heads romaine lettuce

1 cup cornmeal

1 cup all-purpose flour

1 tablespoon Chef Williams Original Cajun Seasoning

4 pounds fresh or frozen squid, bodies cut into 1/2-inch rings

1 1/2 cups shredded Romano or Parmesan cheese

1 5 1/2-ounce package Italian-style croutons

Caesar dressing

Fried shrimp, oysters, or chicken are great substitutes for the squid in this Italian favorite.

COOKING INSTRUCTIONS

1 Preheat oil to 375°F.

2 Rinse lettuce well with cold water; shake off excess. Cut off core and tear lettuce into bite-size pieces. Rinse again with cold water; spin lettuce dry with a salad spinner or pat dry with paper towels. Cover and chill.

3 Combine cornmeal, flour, and Chef Williams Original Cajun Seasoning; stir well with a whisk. Thaw squid, if frozen. Rinse squid; pat dry with paper towels. Place squid rings in a large bowl and sprinkle with cornmeal mixture; toss well.

4 For calamari, fry a handful of squid at a time for 3 minutes or until golden. Remove from hot oil and drain on paper towels.

5 In another bowl combine lettuce, cheese, and croutons; drizzle with desired amount of Caesar dressing. Toss well. Divide salad among 12 plates; top with hot, fried calamari.

Serves 12.

Southern Onion Crab Cakes

Ingredients

- 2 tablespoons butter
- 1 medium onion, thinly sliced
- 1 tablespoon minced garlic
  Oil
- 3 large eggs
- ¼ cup Chef Williams Cajun Garlic Recipe
- 1 teaspoon Chef Williams Original Cajun Seasoning
- ½ teaspoon garlic salt
- 1 pound fresh or frozen lump crabmeat, picked over
- 1½ cups dry bread crumbs
- 1 cup finely crushed buttery crackers
- 1 teaspoon salt
  Green Onion Tartar Sauce (see page 143)

COOKING INSTRUCTIONS

1 Melt butter in a skillet over high heat. Add onion; cook 4 minutes or until onion starts to brown lightly, stirring constantly. Reduce heat to medium; cook 15 to 20 minutes or until onions have lightly caramelized, stirring constantly. Stir in garlic; cook 2 minutes, stirring twice. Set aside; cool completely.

2 Preheat oil to 350°F.

3 Combine eggs and marinade; stir well with a whisk. Add Chef Williams Original Cajun Seasoning and garlic salt; stir well. Thaw crabmeat, if frozen. Rinse crabmeat; pat dry with paper towels. Add bread crumbs, crabmeat, and onion mixture; mix well. Divide mixture into 8 portions. Shape each portion into a 4-inch patty. Combine cracker crumbs and salt; mix well. Roll crab cakes in cracker crumbs, coating well on all sides.

4 Fry 3 or 4 crab cakes at a time for 7 to 8 minutes or until golden. Remove from hot oil and drain on paper towels. Serve warm with Green Onion Tartar Sauce.

Serves 8.

Fried Soft-Shell Crabs

Ingredients

1 dozen fresh or frozen soft-shell
    crabs
  Oil
2 cups all-purpose flour
2 tablespoons Chef Williams
    Original Cajun Seasoning
3 cups packaged pancake mix
4 cups seltzer water

Seasonally, a crab will shed its hard outer shell. When it does, the whole crab is deliciously edible. Soft-shell crabs are generally available from April until September.

COOKING INSTRUCTIONS

1 Thaw crabs, if frozen. Rinse crabs thoroughly in cold water. Remove gills. Turn onto back side, and carefully remove the small pointy apron at the lower part of the shell with a paring knife. Rinse crabs; pat dry with paper towels. Set aside.

2 Preheat oil to 350°F.

3 Combine flour and Chef Williams Original Cajun Seasoning in a bowl; stir well with a whisk. In another bowl combine pancake mix and seltzer water; stir well with a whisk.

4 Dredge crabs in seasoned flour; shake off excess flour. Dip crabs into batter, letting excess batter drain. Dredge again in seasoned flour. Fry 2 or 3 crabs at a time for 5 to 6 minutes or until golden. Remove from hot oil and drain on paper towels.

Serves 12.

Crab Balls

Ingredients

- 3 pounds fresh or frozen crabmeat, picked over
- 1 celery stalk, finely chopped
- ½ cup finely chopped sweet pepper
- 2 green onions, finely chopped
- 1 tablespoon minced garlic
- ½ cup mayonnaise
- 2 tablespoons Chef Williams Cajun Butter Recipe
- 2 tablespoons Creole mustard
- 1 tablespoon hot sauce
- 6 large egg yolks, lightly beaten
- 1½ cups bread crumbs
  Oil
- 2 large eggs
- 1 cup milk
- 2 cups cornstarch
  Easy Rémoulade Sauce
    (see page 149)

COOKING INSTRUCTIONS

1 Combine crabmeat, celery, sweet pepper, green onions, and garlic; mix well. In another bowl combine mayonnaise, marinade, mustard, hot sauce, and egg yolks; stir well with a whisk. Combine crab mixture, mayonnaise mixture, and bread crumbs; mix well.

2 Form mixture into 1-inch balls; place on a baking sheet lined with waxed paper. Cover and chill 2 hours.

3 Preheat oil to 350°F.

4 Combine eggs and milk; beat well with a whisk. Dip balls into egg mixture. Roll in cornstarch, coating well.

5 Fry 8 or 10 crab balls at a time for 3 to 4 minutes or until golden. Remove from heat and drain on paper towels.

6 Serve with Easy Rémoulade Sauce.

Serves 12 to 14.

Chapter 7
Side FRYeds

Buttermilk Hushpuppies

Ingredients

- 2 cups cornmeal
- ½ cup all-purpose flour
- 3 tablespoons sugar
- 2 tablespoons Chef Williams Original Cajun Seasoning
- 1 teaspoon baking soda
- 1 large egg
- 1¼ cups buttermilk
- 1 tablespoon vegetable oil
- 2 cups chopped green onions
- ¼ cup finely chopped jalapeño pepper
- Oil

COOKING INSTRUCTIONS

1 Combine first 5 ingredients in a large bowl; stir well with a whisk. In another bowl beat egg with a whisk. Add buttermilk and 1 tablespoon oil; stir well. Add green onions and jalapeño; stir well. Add egg mixture to cornmeal mixture; stir until just blended. Cover and chill 1 hour.

2 Preheat oil to 350°F.

3 Drop batter by rounded teaspoonfuls into hot oil. Fry 6 or 7 hushpuppies at a time for 4 minutes or until golden, turning once. Remove and drain on paper towels.

Makes 3 to 4 dozen.

Beer Cheese Hushpuppies

Ingredients

- 2 cups self-rising cornmeal
- ½ cup all-purpose flour
- 1 teaspoon Chef Williams Original Cajun Seasoning
- 2 large eggs
- 3 tablespoons packed brown sugar
- ¾ cup ice cold beer
- 2 teaspoons Worcestershire sauce
- ½ cup (6 ounces) finely shredded sharp cheddar cheese
- 2 tablespoons seeded and minced jalapeño pepper
- 1 tablespoon minced garlic
- Oil

COOKING INSTRUCTIONS

1 Combine cornmeal, flour, and Chef Williams Original Cajun Seasoning; stir well with a whisk. In another bowl combine eggs and brown sugar; stir well. Add beer and Worcestershire sauce; stir well. Combine cornmeal mixture and egg mixture; mix well. Stir in cheese, jalapeño, and garlic. Cover and chill 30 minutes.

2 Preheat oil to 375°F.

3 Carefully drop batter by rounded tablespoonfuls into hot oil. Fry 6 or 8 hushpuppies at a time for 1 to 2 minutes or until golden brown. Remove from hot oil and drain on paper towels.

Makes about 4 dozen.

Side FRYeds

Fried Jambalaya Cakes

Ingredients

- ¼ cup butter
- 1 cup finely chopped onions
- ½ cup finely chopped sweet pepper
- 1 tablespoon minced garlic
- 4½ cups chicken broth or water
- 1 teaspoon Chef Williams Original Cajun Seasoning
- 2 cups uncooked converted rice
- 3 large eggs
- 1½ cups all-purpose flour
- Oil

COOKING INSTRUCTIONS

1 Melt butter in a saucepan over medium-high heat. Add onions, sweet pepper, and garlic; cook 4 minutes, stirring constantly. Add chicken broth and Chef Williams Original Cajun Seasoning; stir well. Bring to a boil then stir in rice. Return to a boil; reduce heat. Simmer, covered, 20 minutes or until tender. Remove from heat (do not uncover) and let stand 30 minutes. Cool completely.

2 Combine rice mixture, eggs, and flour; stir well. Using a 2½-inch biscuit cutter or a ½-cup dry measuring cup as a mold, press to form small cakes. Dust with flour. Place cakes on a baking sheet and cover with waxed paper. Chill 30 minutes.

3 Preheat oil to 375°F.

4 Fry 4 or 5 cakes at a time for 3 or 4 minutes or until golden, turning once. Remove from hot oil and drain on paper towels.

Makes 8 cakes.

Fried Pistolettes

Ingredients

Oil

1 14-ounce package (12 rolls)
   French-style pistolettes
   (oblong-shaped brown-and-
   serve rolls)

COOKING INSTRUCTIONS

1 Preheat oil to 350°F.

2 Fry pistolettes 3 or 4 at a time for 1 minute or until golden, turning once. Remove from hot oil and drain on paper towels.

Serves 12.

Old River Asparagus

Ingredients

Oil
1 pound fresh asparagus
1 cup all-purpose flour
¾ cup cornstarch
1½ teaspoons Chef Williams
     Original Cajun Seasoning
1 teaspoon sugar
2 large eggs, beaten
1 cup cold beer

COOKING INSTRUCTIONS

You will really be surprised at the delicious, buttery flavor this recipe generates. I'm not sure what frying does to asparagus, but whatever it is, I'm not complaining.

1 Preheat oil to 325°F.

2 Snap off the tough ends of each asparagus stalk. Peel stem ends with a vegetable peeler.

3 Combine flour, cornstarch, Chef Williams Original Cajun Seasoning, and sugar; stir well. Add eggs and beer; stir until smooth. Dip asparagus in batter.

4 Fry asparagus a few at a time for 1 to 2 minutes or until golden. Remove from hot oil and drain on paper towels.

Serves 6 to 8.

Green Beans and Fried Onions

Ingredients

1 pound fresh green beans
1 small ham hock or 1 beef
    bouillon cube
1 cup water
1 teaspoon Chef Williams
    Original Cajun Seasoning
2 cups Onion Rings (see
    page 129)

COOKING INSTRUCTIONS

1 Rinse green beans with cold water; slice off stem ends. Combine green beans, ham hock, and water in a large pot. Bring to a boil. Reduce heat and simmer, covered, for 10 to 15 minutes or until tender, stirring occasionally. Drain well.

2 In a large bowl combine hot green beans, Chef Williams Original Cajun Seasoning, and hot Onion Rings; toss well. If desired, discard ham hock before serving.

Serves 8.

Zucchini Wheels

Ingredients

- 5 medium zucchini
- 2 cups buttermilk
- Oil
- 1½ cups all-purpose flour
- 1½ cups cornmeal
- 2 teaspoons salt
- ¼ teaspoon ground red pepper

COOKING INSTRUCTIONS

1 Rinse zucchini well with cold water; pat dry with paper towels. Slice crosswise into ½-inch rounds; place in a large bowl. Pour buttermilk over zucchini; cover and chill 1 hour.

2 Preheat oil to 350°F.

3 Combine flour, cornmeal, salt, and pepper; stir well with a whisk. Drain zucchini; discard buttermilk. Dip into flour mixture, coating all sides well.

4 Fry several zucchini wheels at a time for 2 minutes or until golden, turning once. Remove from hot oil and drain on paper towels.

Serves 10.

Fried Portobello Mushrooms

Ingredients

Oil

6 large portobello mushrooms
(about 6 ounces each)

1 cup all-purpose flour

1 tablespoon Chef Williams
Original Cajun Seasoning

1 large egg

1 cup buttermilk

COOKING INSTRUCTIONS

1 Preheat oil to 350°F.

2 Remove and discard stems and gills from mushrooms; cut mushrooms into ½-inch slices. Combine flour and Chef Williams Original Cajun Seasoning; stir well with a whisk. In another bowl combine egg and buttermilk; stir well with a whisk.

3 Dip mushroom slices into egg mixture. Dredge in flour, coating each side well. Fry 6 or 7 mushroom slices at a time for 2 minutes or until golden, turning once.

4 Remove from hot oil and drain on paper towels.

Serves 10 to 12.

Ingredients

- 2 cups Chef Williams Cajun Butter Recipe
- 4 green tomatoes, thinly sliced
  Oil
- 3 large eggs
- ¼ cup milk
- 1 8½-ounce package corn muffin mix
  Chef Williams Original Cajun Seasoning

The secret to frying green tomatoes is to fry them until well done. Pick firm green tomatoes from your garden or farmers' market when in season.

COOKING INSTRUCTIONS

1 **Combine marinade and tomatoes in a large heavy-duty plastic bag; mix well. Squeeze out excess air and seal. Refrigerate for 1 hour.**

2 **Preheat oil to 350°F.**

3 **Combine eggs and milk; stir well with a whisk. Remove tomatoes from marinade and shake off excess marinade. Dip into egg mixture. Dredge in corn muffin mix, coating all sides well.**

4 **Fry 5 or 6 tomatoes at a time in hot oil for 3 to 4 minutes or until dark golden, turning once. Remove from hot oil and drain on paper towels. Sprinkle lightly with Chef Williams Original Cajun Seasoning. Let cool for 2 minutes.**

Serves 10.

Fried Corn on the Cob

Ingredients

Oil
1 package (12 half-ears) frozen
    corn on the cob, thawed
Chef Williams Original Cajun
    Seasoning

COOKING INSTRUCTIONS

1 Preheat oil to 350°F.

2 Fry corn a few at a time in hot oil for 4 minutes, turning once. Remove and drain on paper towels.

3 Sprinkle corn with Chef Williams Original Cajun Seasoning.

Serves 12.

Side FRYeds

Deep Fried Cauliflower

Ingredients

Oil
1 large head cauliflower
    (about 2 pounds)
2 cups dry bread crumbs
1 tablespoon Chef Williams
    Original Cajun Seasoning
3 large eggs
¼ cup milk

COOKING INSTRUCTIONS

1 Preheat oil to 350°F.

2 Remove outer leaves of cauliflower. Rinse with cold water; pat dry with a paper towel. Break into florets.

3 In a small bowl combine bread crumbs and Chef Williams Original Cajun Seasoning; stir well with a whisk. In another small bowl combine eggs and milk; stir well with a whisk. Dip florets into egg mixture. Coat with the bread crumb mixture.

4 Fry florets in batches for 1½ to 2 minutes or until golden. Remove from hot oil and drain on paper towels.

Serves 8 to 10.

Deep Fried Mashed Potatoes

Ingredients

- 2 pounds baking potatoes, peeled and cut in quarters
- 1½ teaspoons salt
- 1 cup milk
- ½ cup butter
- 1½ teaspoons salt
- 1 cup all-purpose flour
- 3 large eggs
- ½ cup half-and-half
- Oil
- 1 cup fine dry bread crumbs
- 1 tablespoon Chef Williams Original Cajun Seasoning
- 2 large eggs
- 2 tablespoons milk
- ½ cup all-purpose flour

COOKING INSTRUCTIONS

1 Pour cold water to 1 inch above potatoes in a large pot. Stir in 1½ teaspoons salt. Bring to a boil; reduce heat and simmer, uncovered, 15 minutes or until fork-tender. Drain well. Mash potatoes with a potato masher, potato ricer, or with the back of a large spoon.

2 Combine milk, butter, and 1½ teaspoons salt in a saucepan over medium heat. Bring to a boil; add flour and immediately stir vigorously with a wooden spoon. Cook mixture, stirring constantly, until a dough ball is formed and starts to pull away from sides of saucepan. Remove from heat; let stand 5 minutes. Add 3 eggs, 1 at a time, stirring until dough is smooth. Add potatoes and half-and-half; stir until smooth. Let mixture cool completely.

3 Preheat oil to 375°F.

4 Combine bread crumbs and Chef Williams Original Cajun Seasoning; stir well with a whisk. In another bowl, combine the 2 eggs and the 2 tablespoons milk; beat well with a whisk. Form potato dough into 2-inch balls. Roll balls lightly in flour; shake off excess. Dip into egg mixture and roll in bread crumbs, coating all sides.

5 Fry a few potato balls at a time for 7 to 8 minutes or until potato balls float or pop.

Serves 8 to 10.

Ingredients

Oil

10 medium Idaho baking potatoes
    (about 4 pounds)

Chef Williams Original Cajun
    Seasoning or salt

Ketchup, mayonnaise, or malt
    vinegar

French fries, also known as "pommes frittes," really started in Belgium. This recipe is very similar to that of the stands selling pommes frites found on the streets of Belgium. They are traditionally served with mayonnaise.

COOKING INSTRUCTIONS

1 Preheat oil to 325°F.

2 Peel potatoes, if desired; cut lengthwise into ¼-inch-wide sticks. Fry 2 handfuls of potatoes at a time for 2 minutes or until lightly golden. Remove with a slotted spoon and drain on paper towels (potatoes can sit at room temperature for up to 2 hours after first frying).

3 Heat oil to 400°F.

4 Fry a handful of potatoes at a time for 4 minutes or until golden and crisp. Remove with a slotted spoon and drain on paper towels. In a large bowl toss fries with **Chef Williams Original Cajun Seasoning.** Serve with ketchup, mayonnaise, or malt vinegar.

Serves 10 to 15.

French Fried Potatoes

Ingredients

Oil

6 10-ounce Idaho baking
    potatoes

1 tablespoon salt

    Chef Williams Original Cajun
    Seasoning

COOKING INSTRUCTIONS

1 Preheat oil to 350°F.

2 Peel potatoes; cut into ⅜-inch-wide sticks. Cover potato sticks with cold water. Sprinkle with salt; stir well.

3 Drain potatoes well. Fry a handful of potatoes at a time for 5 minutes or until crisp. Remove from hot oil and drain on paper towels. Sprinkle with Chef Williams Original Cajun Seasoning.

Serves 10 to 12.

Side FRYeds

Sweet Potato Fries

Ingredients

Oil
½ cup sugar
1 teaspoon ground cinnamon
6 medium sweet potatoes
    (about 10 ounces each)

COOKING INSTRUCTIONS

1 Preheat oil to 350°F.

2 Combine sugar and cinnamon; mix well. Peel sweet potatoes and cut into ⅜-inch-wide sticks. Fry a handful of potatoes at a time for 3 to 5 minutes or until golden, turning once.

3 Remove from hot oil and drain on paper towels. Sprinkle with cinnamon sugar.

Serves 10 to 12.

Fried Potato Salad

Ingredients

- 6 large eggs
- Oil
- 1 pound bacon
- 4 pounds red potatoes
- Chef Williams Original Cajun Seasoning
- 1½ cups mayonnaise
- ½ cup dill pickle relish

COOKING INSTRUCTIONS

1 Cover eggs with 1 inch cold water in a large pot. Place over medium-high heat. Bring to a boil. Cover and remove from heat. Let stand 15 to 17 minutes. Drain water. Run cold water over eggs until completely cool. Peel and chop eggs; set aside.

2 Preheat oil to 350°F.

3 Separate bacon strips. Carefully lower each piece of bacon into hot oil; fry for 1 minute or until crisp. Remove from hot oil and drain on paper towels. Crumble; set aside.

4 Scrub potatoes; rinse with cold water. Cut into 1-inch cubes. Fry potatoes in batches for 5 minutes or until tender and golden. Remove from hot oil and drain on paper towels.

5 Place warm potatoes in a large bowl. Sprinkle with Chef Williams Original Cajun Seasoning; toss well. Add crumbled bacon, chopped egg, mayonnaise, and relish; toss until potatoes are well coated.

Serves 12.

Side FRYeds

Ingredients

Oil

8 small baking potatoes
  (about 2 pounds)

Chef Williams Original Cajun
  Seasoning or salt

Green Onion Tartar Sauce (see
  page 143)

COOKING INSTRUCTIONS

1 Preheat oil to 375°F.

2 Peel potatoes, if desired. Slice thinly using a sharp knife, a cheese slicer, or slicing feature of a food processor. Cover sliced potatoes with cold water until all potatoes are sliced. Drain potatoes well.

3 Fry potato slices a few at a time for 1 to 2 minutes or until golden and crisp, turning once. Remove from hot oil and drain on paper towels. Sprinkle with Chef Williams Original Cajun Seasoning. Serve with Green Onion Tartar Sauce.

Serves 10 to 12.

Onion Rings

Ingredients

Oil

3 large Vidalia onions or other sweet onions

2 cups flour

2 tablespoons Chef Williams Original Cajun Seasoning

COOKING INSTRUCTIONS

1 Preheat oil to 350°F.

2 Carefully slice onions thinly with a sharp knife. Combine flour and Chef Williams Original Cajun Seasoning; mix well. Sprinkle seasoned flour over onions until nicely coated; mix thoroughly.

3 Sprinkle onions, a handful at a time, over hot oil. Fry 3 to 4 minutes or until golden. Remove from hot oil and drain on paper towels.

Serves 6 to 8.

Side FRYeds

Baked Beans

Ingredients

- 8 slices bacon
- 1 large onion, finely chopped
- 1 tablespoon minced garlic
- 1 tablespoon minced jalapeño pepper
- 3 16-ounce cans navy beans, undrained
- ½ cup firmly packed dark brown sugar
- 1 cup bottled chili sauce
- 2 tablespoons Creole mustard
- 1 tablespoon Chef Williams Cajun Garlic Recipe
- 1 tablespoon Chef Williams Original Cajun Seasoning

COOKING INSTRUCTIONS

1 Preheat oven to 350°F.

2 Cook bacon in a large skillet until brown and crisp. Remove bacon and drain on paper towels; reserve 2 tablespoons bacon drippings in skillet. Cool bacon and crumble.

3 Add onion to bacon drippings; cook and stir over medium heat for 10 minutes or until nicely browned. Add garlic and jalapeño; cook and stir 2 minutes. Stir in navy beans, brown sugar, chili sauce, Creole mustard, marinade, and Chef Williams Original Cajun Seasoning. Bring to a simmer, stirring constantly. Remove from heat.

4 Spoon mixture into a lightly greased 13×9-inch baking dish. Sprinkle with crumbled bacon. Bake for 45 minutes or until bubbly.

Serves 10.

Creamy Coleslaw

Ingredients

- 1 head green cabbage, finely shredded (about 2 pounds)
- 1 large carrot, peeled and finely grated
- 1 small green sweet pepper, finely chopped
- 1 small red sweet pepper, finely chopped
- 1 celery stalk, finely chopped
- 3 green onions, thinly sliced
- ¾ cup mayonnaise
- ¼ cup sour cream
- 2 tablespoons Creole mustard
- 2 tablespoons sugar
- 2 tablespoons apple cider vinegar
- 1 teaspoon salt
- 1 teaspoon hot sauce

COOKING INSTRUCTIONS

In a large bowl combine cabbage, carrot, sweet peppers, celery, and green onions; toss well. For dressing, in another bowl combine mayonnaise, sour cream, mustard, sugar, vinegar, salt, and hot sauce; stir well. Drizzle dressing over cabbage mixture; toss until well coated.

Serves 10.

Chapter 8
Saucy Sauces and Tongue Tinglers

Sweet Creole Mustard Cream

Ingredients

4 cups heavy cream
⅔ cup Creole mustard
¼ cup honey

This is a rich sauce that should only glaze meats and vegetables.

COOKING INSTRUCTIONS

1 Bring cream to a boil over high heat. Reduce heat to medium-low heat and simmer, uncovered, for 35 to 60 minutes* or until mixture is reduced to 1 cup, stirring often.

2 Remove from heat. Add mustard and honey; stir until smooth.

Makes about 1¾ cups.

***Note: Reduction times may vary.**

Vegetable Dip

Ingredients

- 1 cup mayonnaise
- 2 teaspoons Chef Williams Cajun Garlic Recipe
- 1 teaspoon prepared horseradish

COOKING INSTRUCTIONS

1 Combine mayonnaise, marinade, and horseradish in a bowl; stir well with whisk until smooth.

2 Cover and chill 1 hour.

Makes 2¼ cups.

Wasabi Marmalade

Ingredients

- 2 to 3 tablespoons dry wasabi powder
- 3 tablespoons rice wine vinegar
- 2 cups orange marmalade

COOKING INSTRUCTIONS

1 Combine desired amount of wasabi powder and rice wine vinegar; let stand 10 minutes.

2 Add orange marmalade; stir well.

Makes about 2 cups.

Boutte's Eatin' Sauce

Ingredients

COOKING INSTRUCTIONS

- 2 pounds onions, chopped
- 10 ounces cooking oil
- 1 6-ounce can tomato paste
- 3 cups water
- 1 16-ounce bottle ketchup
- ¼ cup Chef Williams Cajun Garlic Recipe
- ¼ cup sugar
- 2 tablespoons hot sauce
- 1 tablespoon mustard

Durwood Boutte, a very close Cajun friend of my dad, gave me this recipe. Just drizzle it over any type of meat and enjoy a truly "kicked up" version of your food.

Cook and stir onions in cooking oil until wilted. Add tomato paste and cook for several minutes. Add water and blend well. Add ketchup, marinade, sugar, hot sauce, and mustard; simmer about 30 minutes. (It doesn't hurt to cook longer.)

Makes about 2 cups.

Saucy Sauces and Tongue Tinglers

Fresh Tomato Salsa

Ingredients

- 1 medium onion, chopped
- 2 large ripe tomatoes, chopped
- 4 jalapeño peppers, seeded and chopped
- 1 tablespoon minced garlic
- ⅓ cup fresh lime juice
- ¼ cup extra-virgin olive oil
- ½ teaspoon salt
- ½ teaspoon hot sauce

COOKING INSTRUCTIONS

Combine onion, tomatoes, jalapeño peppers, garlic, lime juice, olive oil, salt, and hot sauce in a bowl; stir well. Let stand 1 hour.

Serves 12 to 16.

Simple Dipping Sauce

Ingredients

- 1 cup mayonnaise
- ⅓ cup ketchup
- ⅓ cup bottled chili sauce
- 2 tablespoons Chef Williams Cajun Butter Recipe
- 1 tablespoon Worcestershire sauce
- 1 tablespoon Creole mustard
- ¾ cup minced onion
- 1 tablespoon minced garlic
- 2 teaspoons Chef Williams Original Cajun Seasoning
- ½ cup olive oil

COOKING INSTRUCTIONS

1 Combine mayonnaise, ketchup, chili sauce, marinade, Worcestershire sauce, and mustard in a bowl, whisking well. Stir in onion, garlic, and Chef Williams Original Cajun Seasoning.

2 Add oil, 1 tablespoon at a time, whisking well after each tablespoon. Refrigerate until serving.

Makes 2⅓ cups.

Creamy Dill Sauce

Ingredients

- 1 cup sour cream
- 1 cup mayonnaise
- 2 tablespoons minced green onion
- 2 tablespoons minced fresh dill
- 2 tablespoons lemon juice

COOKING INSTRUCTIONS

Combine sour cream, mayonnaise, green onion, dill, and lemon juice in a bowl; stir well with a whisk until smooth. Cover and chill 1 hour.

Makes about 2 cups.

Sweet Potato Relish

Ingredients

- 1 8-ounce sweet potato
- ½ cup minced green onions
- 2 teaspoons grated fresh ginger
- 2 tablespoons fresh apple cider
- 2 tablespoons apple cider vinegar
- 1 teaspoon hot sauce
- ¾ teaspoon salt
- 1 large apple, finely chopped

Sweet potatoes are a very common staple in many diets in Southern Louisiana. If you are lucky enough to live where fresh apple cider can be bought, then take full advantage of the fresh, crisp flavor. Apple juice concentrate works well as a substitute.

COOKING INSTRUCTIONS

1 Preheat oven to 400°F.

2 Bake sweet potato for 1 hour. Remove from oven and cool completely. Spoon out pulp; discard jacket (Sweet potato can be boiled until softened, if desired.)

3 Combine green onions, ginger, cider, vinegar, hot sauce, and salt with sweet potato; stir well. Gently fold in apple.

4 Cover and chill 1 hour.

Makes 2½ cups.

Saucy Sauces and Tongue Tinglers

Front Porch Tartar Sauce

Ingredients

- 1 cup mayonnaise
- 1 medium onion, grated
- 1 teaspoon sweet pickle relish

COOKING INSTRUCTIONS

This tartar sauce recipe has been in my dad's "recipe notes" since 1963. I remember making it when I was a child and he was feeding the Clinton High School (Louisiana) football team after they won the State Championship title.

Combine mayonnaise, onion, and relish in a bowl; stir well with a whisk until smooth. Cover and chill 1 hour.

Makes 1½ cups.

Green Onion Tartar Sauce

Ingredients

- 2 bunches green onions (green tops only), coarsely chopped
- 2 large garlic cloves
- 1½ cups mayonnaise
- ½ cup sour cream
- 1 tablespoon lemon juice
- 1 teaspoon salt
- 1½ teaspoons hot sauce

COOKING INSTRUCTIONS

1 Combine green onions, garlic, mayonnaise, sour cream, lemon juice, salt, and hot sauce in a food processor or blender; process or blend until smooth.

2 Cover and chill 30 minutes.

Makes 2½ cups.

Williams' House Tartar Sauce

Ingredients

1½ cups mayonnaise
½ cup pickle relish
3 tablespoons chopped fresh
    parsley
1 tablespoon Creole mustard
1 tablespoon Chef Williams
    Cajun Butter Recipe

COOKING INSTRUCTIONS

Combine mayonnaise, relish, parsley, mustard, and marinade in a bowl; stir well. Cover and chill 1 hour.

Makes 2 cups.

Cajun Garlic Mayonnaise

Ingredients

- 2 green onions (green tops only), minced
- 2 tablespoons minced garlic
- 2 tablespoons butter, melted
- 2 teaspoons lemon juice
- 1 teaspoon hot sauce
- 1 teaspoon Chef Williams Original Cajun Seasoning
- 2 cups mayonnaise

COOKING INSTRUCTIONS

1 Cook and stir green onions and garlic in melted butter over medium heat for 3 to 4 minutes, stirring constantly. Remove from heat; cool completely.

2 Combine green onion mixture, lemon juice, hot sauce, Chef Williams Original Cajun Seasoning, and mayonnaise in a bowl; stir well with a wire whisk.

Makes about 2 cups.

Cajun Red Sauce

Ingredients

- 1 cup chili sauce
- 1 cup ketchup
- 2 tablespoons Chef Williams Cajun Garlic Recipe
- 2 tablespoons prepared horseradish
- 1 tablespoon hot sauce
- 1 teaspoon salt
- 1 teaspoon dry mustard
- 1 teaspoon black pepper

COOKING INSTRUCTIONS

Combine chili sauce, ketchup, marinade, horseradish, hot sauce, salt, mustard, and pepper in a bowl; stir well with a whisk until smooth. Cover and chill 1 hour.

Makes 2½ cups.

Cocktail Sauce

Ingredients

2 cups ketchup
1 tablespoon hot sauce
1 tablespoon Chef Williams
    Cajun Garlic Recipe

COOKING INSTRUCTIONS

Combine ketchup, hot sauce, and marinade in a bowl; stir well with a whisk until smooth. Cover and chill 1 hour.

Makes 2 cups.

Ingredients

- 4 cups minced Vidalia onion or other sweet yellow onion
- 6 tablespoons butter, melted
- 1 tablespoon minced garlic
- 1 10-ounce can beef broth
- ¾ cup Chef Williams Cajun Butter Recipe
- ¼ cup warm honey
- 2 tablespoons Creole mustard
- ½ teaspoon salt

COOKING INSTRUCTIONS

1 Cook and stir onions in melted butter over high heat for 5 minutes, stirring constantly. Reduce heat to medium. Cook and stir 15 to 20 minutes or until lightly caramelized, stirring constantly. Add garlic; cook and stir 1 minute. Add broth and marinade. Bring to a boil.

2 Reduce heat and simmer, uncovered, for 10 minutes or until mixture is reduced to 1½ cups. Add honey, mustard, and salt; stir well.

3 Cover and chill 1 hour.

Makes about 1¾ cups.

Ingredients

- 3 tablespoons horseradish
- 3 cloves garlic, chopped
- ½ cup Creole mustard
- 1 small onion, chopped
- 4 celery leaves, chopped
- 2 tablespoons paprika
- 3 sprigs fresh parsley, chopped
- 1 cup olive oil
- 1 ounce Chef Williams Cajun Garlic Recipe

Serve over boiled shellfish on a bed of lettuce.

COOKING INSTRUCTIONS

Combine horseradish, garlic, mustard, onion, celery leaves, paprika, parsley, olive oil, and marinade in a bowl; stir well.

Serves 6.

Rémoulade Sauce

Ingredients

- ½ cup mayonnaise
- 2 tablespoons prepared horseradish
- 2 tablespoons lemon juice
- 2 tablespoons ketchup
- 2 tablespoons Worcestershire sauce
- 2 tablespoons dried, minced onion
- 1 tablespoon Creole mustard
- 1 tablespoon apple cider vinegar
- 1 tablespoon hot sauce
- 1 tablespoon minced garlic
- 1 tablespoon dried parsley, crushed
- 2 teaspoons sweet paprika
- 1 teaspoon salt

COOKING INSTRUCTIONS

1 Combine all ingredients in a bowl; stir well with a whisk.

2 Cover and chill 1 hour.

Makes 1½ cups.

J. B.'s Potato Sauce

Ingredients

- 2 large yellow onions, thinly sliced
- 8 ounces bottled Italian salad dressing
- 3 ounces Chef Williams Cajun Butter Recipe
- ¼ cup cider vinegar
- 1 lemon, sliced
- ½ cup water

COOKING INSTRUCTIONS

JB (Jeanne Belzons) is my mom. Her potato sauce recipe was developed as a dipping sauce for potatoes cooked along with crawfish in a pot of boiling seasoned water. Her sauce adds so much flavor to the potatoes you may want to just eat the potatoes and give the crawfish to someone else.

Combine all ingredients in large pot and simmer over medium heat until onions are wilted and liquid has been reduced to about one-fourth.

Serves 10.

Ingredients

 COOKING INSTRUCTIONS

- 1 tablespoon olive oil
- 1 tablespoon minced garlic
- 4 14½-ounce cans crushed tomatoes
- 1 tablespoon sugar
- 2 teaspoons Chef Williams Original Cajun Seasoning
- 1 teaspoon dried oregano, crushed
- ½ teaspoon dried basil, crushed
- 2 bay leaves

1 Heat oil in a skillet over medium heat. Add garlic; cook and stir 1 minute. Add remaining ingredients; stir well.

2 Bring to a boil; reduce heat and simmer, uncovered, for 30 minutes or until liquid is almost evaporated, stirring often. Discard bay leaves.

Makes about 4 cups.

Sauce Maurice

Ingredients

1 cup barbecue sauce
½ cup prepared horseradish
1 tablespoon hot sauce

COOKING INSTRUCTIONS

Enjoy as a finishing sauce when grilling pork, chicken, or beef. Apply it just a few minutes prior to removing your meat from the grill.

Combine barbecue sauce, horseradish, and hot sauce in a bowl; stir well. Chill.

Enjoy as a finishing sauce when grilling pork, chicken, or beef. Apply it just a few minutes prior to removing your meat from the grill.

Makes 1½ cups.

Saucy Sauces and Tongue Tinglers

Cajun Cream Gravy

Ingredients

2 tablespoons butter
2 tablespoons all-purpose flour
1 cup chicken broth
½ cup heavy cream
½ cup Chef Williams Cajun
    Butter Recipe
¾ teaspoon Chef Williams
    Original Cajun Seasoning
½ teaspoon dried oregano
½ cup grated Parmesan cheese

COOKING INSTRUCTIONS

To make a roux, melt butter in a saucepan over medium-high heat. Stir in flour until smooth. Cook 1 minute, stirring constantly. Combine broth, cream, and marinade. Slowly add to roux, stirring until smooth. Stir in Chef Williams Original Cajun Seasoning and oregano. Bring to boil. Reduce heat to medium low and simmer, uncovered, stirring constantly until thickened. Stir in Parmesan cheese.

Makes 1½ cups.

Cajun Gravy

Ingredients

- 2 tablespoons butter
- ¼ pound finely chopped tasso or Cajun smoked sausage
- 2 tablespoons all-purpose flour
- 1 tablespoon tomato paste
- 2 10½-ounce cans beef broth
- ¾ cup Chef Williams Cajun Garlic Recipe
- ½ teaspoon dried oregano
- ¼ teaspoon dried thyme, crushed

COOKING INSTRUCTIONS

1 Melt butter in a saucepan over medium-high heat.

2 Add tasso or sausage; cook 3 minutes, stirring constantly. Sprinkle flour evenly over meat; cook 2 minutes, stirring constantly.

3 Add tomato paste, broth, marinade, oregano, and thyme; stir well.

4 Bring to a boil; reduce heat to medium low and simmer, uncovered, for 15 minutes, stirring constantly until thickened.

Makes 2 cups.

 Red Hot Barbecue Sauce

Ingredients

  COOKING INSTRUCTIONS

½ cup packed dark brown sugar
1 6-ounce can tomato paste
½ cup strong brewed coffee
½ cup Chef Williams Cajun
   Butter Recipe
½ cup cider vinegar
1 tablespoon hot sauce
1 tablespoon Worcestershire
   sauce
1 teaspoon Chef Williams
   Original Cajun Seasoning
½ teaspoon onion powder
½ teaspoon garlic powder
1 orange, juiced

1 Combine brown sugar, tomato paste, coffee, and marinade in a saucepan over medium heat.

2 Bring to a boil; reduce heat to low and simmer 5 minutes, stirring constantly.

3 Stir in remaining ingredients. Simmer 15 minutes, stirring often. Strain well.

Makes about 2 cups.

Homemade Tomato Ketchup

Ingredients

- ¼ cup butter
- 4 cups minced Vidalia or other sweet onion
- 2 tablespoons minced garlic
- 7 pounds vine-ripened tomatoes, peeled, seeded, and chopped
- ⅔ cup firmly packed brown sugar
- 1¼ cups apple cider vinegar
- ½ cup Chef Williams Cajun Butter Recipe
- 1 tablespoon Creole mustard
- ⅛ teaspoon ground cloves
- ⅛ teaspoon ground allspice
- 1 teaspoon celery salt

It's hard to replace store-bought ketchup, but when fresh vine-ripe tomatoes are in season, this classic makes a great sauce to go with everything fried. This recipe is difficult and takes a lot of attention because it gets real thick and can burn easily if not constantly stirred over medium-low heat. If it starts to burn on the bottom, do not continue to stir; immediately remove from heat and transfer to another pot. Resume cooking. If burned residue on the bottom of the pot is stirred into the ketchup, the flavor will taste burned.

COOKING INSTRUCTIONS

1 Melt butter in a large heavy pot over medium-high heat. Add onions; cook and stir 10 minutes. Add garlic and tomatoes; stir well. Bring to a boil; cover, reduce heat and simmer, covered, for 20 minutes, stirring occasionally. Process mixture in a food processor, blender, or food mill until smooth.

2 Combine tomato mixture, brown sugar, vinegar, marinade, and Creole mustard; stir well. Bring to a boil; reduce heat to low and simmer, uncovered. Stir constantly for 30 to 40 minutes or until mixture reaches a ketchup consistency. Stir constantly while scraping along the bottom of pot to prevent burning.

3 Stir in cloves, allspice, and celery salt. Cover and chill overnight. Ketchup will keep up to 2 weeks in the refrigerator.

Makes about 2 cups.

Saucy Sauces and Tongue Tinglers

Chapter 8
FRYed Sweetness

Apple Fritters

Ingredients

Oil
2½ cups all-purpose flour
1 tablespoon baking powder
½ cup sugar
2 teaspoons cinnamon
1 teaspoon salt
4 large egg yolks
½ cup milk
½ cup apple cider, hard cider, or
   apple juice
2 cups chopped apple or pear
2 egg whites
Apple Cider Glaze (see
   page 175)

COOKING INSTRUCTIONS

1 Preheat oil to 350°F.

2 In a medium bowl combine flour, baking powder, sugar, cinnamon, and salt; stir well with a whisk. In another bowl combine egg yolks, milk, and apple cider; stir well with a whisk. Combine flour mixture, egg mixture, and apple; stir well.

3 In a clean bowl beat egg whites with a whisk until stiff peaks form; gently fold into batter.

4 Spoon batter by rounded tablespoonfuls into hot oil. Fry 4 or 5 fritters at a time for 4 to 5 minutes or until golden, turning once. Remove from hot oil and drain on paper towels. Dip into Apple Cider Glaze. Serve warm.

Serves 10 to 12.

Beignets and Café au Lait

Ingredients

- 1 package active dry yeast
- ¼ cup warm water (105°F to 115°F)
- 2 cups all-purpose flour
- ¼ cup sugar
- ¾ teaspoon salt
- 3 tablespoons cold lard or vegetable shortening
- ½ cup buttermilk
- ¼ cup water
- 1 large egg
  - Oil
  - Powdered sugar

Café au Lait
- 4 cups hot strong brewed coffee with chicory
- 3 cups hot milk

COOKING INSTRUCTIONS

1 Sprinkle yeast over warm water; let stand 5 minutes. Set aside. In a medium bowl combine flour, sugar, and salt; stir well with a whisk. Add lard in small pieces; mix well, squeezing mixture in palms of hands until lard is incorporated.

2 In another bowl combine buttermilk, water, and egg; beat well with a whisk. Combine flour mixture and buttermilk mixture; mix until dry ingredients are moistened and a soft dough forms. Knead 2 minutes or until smooth. Do not overwork dough.

3 Place in a well greased bowl. Turn once to coat. Cover with a damp towel and let rise in a warm place, free from drafts, for 40 to 45 minutes or until doubled in size.

4 Turn dough onto a floured surface; gently pat or roll to a ½-inch thickness. Cut into 2½-inch squares. Let rise 30 more minutes.

5 Preheat oil to 350°F.

6 Fry beignets for 1 minute on each side or until golden. Remove from hot oil and drain on paper towels. Generously dust with powdered sugar.

7 For Café au Lait, combine hot coffee and hot milk; stir well. Serve immediately with hot beignets.

Serves 12.

FRYed Sweetness

Strawberry Fried Shortcake

Ingredients

Oil
1 16-ounce loaf angel food cake
1 16-ounce package frozen
    sweetened, sliced
    strawberries, thawed
1 6-ounce container frozen
    whipped topping, thawed
Powdered sugar

A surprising way to prepare the desert classic, it's a delicious alternative. Use fresh oil for frying the cake because its delicate taste would be altered by other flavors in used oil.

COOKING INSTRUCTIONS

1 Preheat oil to 350°F.

2 Cut cake into twelve 1-inch slices. Fry 3 or 4 slices at a time for 1 minute, turning once. Remove from hot oil and drain on paper towels. Cool completely. Place each slice on a dessert plate. Evenly top each piece of cake with strawberries; top with a dollop of whipped topping. Dust with powdered sugar.

Serves 12.

Pear and Blue Cheese Phyllo Wrap

Ingredients

- 2 large Bartlett pears, peeled, cored, and chopped
- ¼ cup granulated sugar
- ¼ cup firmly packed brown sugar
- ¼ teaspoon ground cinnamon
- 2 tablespoons balsamic vinegar
- 1 teaspoon vanilla
- 6 sheets phyllo dough
- ½ cup butter, melted
- 9 ounces crumbled blue cheese
  Oil
- 6 tablespoons powdered sugar
  Caramel Cream Sauce
     (see page 178)

COOKING INSTRUCTIONS

1 In a medium saucepan combine pears, sugar, brown sugar, cinnamon, balsamic vinegar, and vanilla; mix well. Bring to a simmer; cook 30 to 35 minutes or until almost dry, stirring constantly. Cool completely.

2 On a clean surface lay down 1 sheet phyllo dough; lightly brush with butter. Top with 1 more sheet phyllo dough; lightly brush with butter. Spoon a third of the filling in center of phyllo. Sprinkle a third of the blue cheese evenly over filling. Fold top corner over filling, tucking tip of corner under filling; fold left and right corners over filling. Brush remaining corner lightly with butter; tightly roll filled end toward remaining corner and gently press to seal. Repeat procedure twice with remaining ingredients.

3 Preheat oil to 325°F.

4 Fry wraps 4 to 6 minutes or until golden, turning once. Remove from hot oil and drain on paper towels. Sprinkle with powdered sugar. Slice in half on a bias. Serve warm with Caramel Cream Sauce.

Serves 6.

FRYed Sweetness

Funnel Cake

Ingredients

Oil
1 cup powdered sugar
1 tablespoon ground cinnamon
3 cups all-purpose flour
1½ tablespoons baking powder
1 teaspoon salt
½ cup granulated sugar
2 large eggs
1 egg yolk
2¼ cups milk
1 teaspoon vanilla

COOKING INSTRUCTIONS

1 Preheat oil to 375°F.

2 Combine powdered sugar and cinnamon; stir well with a whisk. Set aside.

3 Combine flour, baking powder, salt, and sugar in a large bowl; stir well with a whisk. In another bowl combine eggs, egg yolk, milk, and vanilla; beat well with a whisk. Combine flour mixture and egg mixture; mix well. Pour batter into a large pitcher, pastry bag, squeeze bottle, or other creative container that pours easily.

4 In a slow steady stream pour batter into hot oil in a slow circular motion. Fry 1 cake at a time for 45 seconds to 1 minute, turning once. Remove from hot oil and drain on paper towels. Dust with powdered sugar mixture.

Serves 20.

Fried Ricotta Puffs

Ingredients

Oil
1 16-ounce carton ricotta cheese
2 tablespoons sugar
1 teaspoon ground cinnamon
1 teaspoon grated lemon peel
2 teaspoons self-rising flour
Powdered sugar

Scented with lemon and cinnamon, this pastrylike dessert is out of this world!

COOKING INSTRUCTIONS

1 Preheat oil to 350°F.

2 Combine ricotta cheese, sugar, cinnamon, and lemon peel in a bowl; stir well. Sprinkle with flour; stir well.

3 Drop batter by rounded tablespoonfuls into hot oil. Fry 6 or 7 puffs at a time for 4 minutes or until golden, turning once. Remove and drain on paper towels. Dust with powdered sugar. Serve warm.

Serves 12.

Blackberry Chimichangas

Ingredients

Oil
5 cups fresh or frozen
blackberries, thawed
½ cup granulated sugar
2 tablespoons lemon juice
1½ teaspoons cornstarch
10 10-inch flour tortillas
Wooden toothpicks
Powdered sugar
Vanilla-Bourbon Sauce
(see page 179)

COOKING INSTRUCTIONS

1 Preheat oil to 350°F.

2 Combine blackberries, sugar, lemon juice, and cornstarch in a bowl; toss well. Place 1 tortilla flat on a clean surface, place ½ cup blackberry mixture in center. Fold bottom edge over filling; fold sides over filling. Roll up and secure with a wooden toothpick. Repeat.

3 Fry 2 or 3 chimichangas at a time for 3 to 4 minutes or until golden. Remove from hot oil and drain on paper towels.

4 Dust with powdered sugar. Serve warm with Vanilla-Bourbon Sauce.

Serves 10.

Ice Cream Sundae Buffet

Ingredients

Oil

1 package 8-inch flour tortillas

⅓ cup water

2 cups sifted powdered sugar

½ cup small multicolored
    decorative sprinkles

6 1-cup servings of each desired
    topping*
    Chocolate-Cherry Sauce
    (see page 177)

1 can pressurized whipped
    dessert topping

2 ½-gallon containers ice cream
    of different flavors

The tortillas become the ice cream dish with a fun candy border around the top. They are great for parties and family holiday gatherings.

COOKING INSTRUCTIONS

1 Preheat oil to 350°F.

2 Secure 1 flour tortilla at a time in a small fry basket mold, or place in bottom of a small wire mesh strainer to form a bowl. Fry tortillas 45 seconds to 1 minute or until golden. Remove from hot oil and drain on paper towels. Repeat with remaining tortillas. Cool completely.

3 Combine water and powdered sugar in a large shallow bowl; mix well. Place decorative sprinkles in another shallow bowl. Dip top border of fried tortilla bowl into powdered sugar glaze. Dip into decorative sprinkles. Set aside.

4 Place each topping and sauce into small serving dishes or bowls. Arrange bowls and whipped topping on a table or counter. Fill each decorated tortilla bowl with 1 scoop of each ice cream. Sprinkle with desired toppings.

Serves 8.

Toppings can include, but are not limited to, chopped homemade desserts (such as brownies, cookies, cake crumbles), candy coated milk chocolate or peanut butter pieces, chopped candy bars, chopped cookies, chopped nuts, packaged cereal, chopped fresh, dried or canned fruit, thawed frozen fruit, marshmallows, granola, flaked coconut, etc.

FRYed Sweetness

Fried Ice Cream

Ingredients

1 quart vanilla ice cream
1 cup finely chopped pecans
3 large eggs, beaten well
2 cups finely crushed vanilla
    wafers
  Oil
  Easy Chocolate Sauce (see
      page 176), Vanilla-Bourbon
      Sauce (see page 179), or
      Caramel Cream Sauce (see
      page 178)

It is possible to deep-fry ice cream because you are only frying the outside and making a crisp crust. Be sure to heat the oil back to the desired temperature after each frying. It is similar to dropping an ice cube into a glass of water; the temperature will decrease. You have to maintain 375°F for this recipe to work correctly.

COOKING INSTRUCTIONS

1 Make room in your freezer for a baking sheet. Line baking sheet with waxed paper. Scoop ice cream into eight ½-cup ice cream balls. Quickly roll each ball in pecans, covering all sides well. Place on cookie sheet; freeze 3 hours.

2 Dip each ball in egg. Roll into crushed vanilla wafers, covering all sides well. Freeze 3 hours more.

3 Preheat oil to 375°F.

4 Once oil is hot enough, remove 2 or 3 ice cream balls from freezer. Fry 30 to 45 seconds or until coating is crisp. Remove from hot oil and drain on paper towels. Repeat procedure. Serve immediately with a dessert sauce of your choice.

Serves 8.

Fried Fruit-Filled Pies

Ingredients

- 1 14-ounce can apple pie filling
- 2 8-ounce packages refrigerated crescent rolls, cold
-    Oil
- 2 cups powdered sugar
- ¼ cup milk

This treat can also be made with canned cherry or blueberry filling.

COOKING INSTRUCTIONS

1 Using a potato masher or back of a large spoon, mash apples into small pieces; set aside.

2 Unroll cold dough onto a lightly floured surface, working with only one can at a time. Separate each piece into 2 rectangles along perforations; cut each piece in half (this will give you eight 4-inch squares per roll). Seal perforations on both sides, using fingers.

3 Place 1 tablespoon filling onto half of each dough square. Moisten edges with just a little water; fold dough over filling. Press edges to seal; crimp edges with a fork. Repeat procedure with remaining dough and filling. Freeze pies for 10 minutes.

4 Preheat oil to 350°F.

5 For glaze combine powdered sugar and milk; stir well with a whisk until smooth.

6 Fry 3 or 4 pies at a time for 3 to 4 minutes or until golden, turning once. Remove from hot oil and drain on paper towels. Dip both sides of pies in glaze. Serve warm.

Serves 16.

Ingredients

Oil

2 12¼-ounce packages
refrigerated cinnamon rolls
with icing

2½- to 3-inch star shaped
cookie cutter

2 tablespoons sugar

2 teaspoons cinnamon

COOKING INSTRUCTIONS

1 Preheat oil to 350°F.

2 Remove cinnamon roll dough from package; reserve icing container. Separate dough into individual rolls; flatten each roll with palm of hand. Using a 2½- to 3-inch star shape cookie cutter, cut dough into shapes. Lightly twist each point.

3 Fry a few rolls at a time for 3 to 4 minutes, turning once. Remove from hot oil and drain on paper towels.

4 Stir together sugar and cinnamon. Evenly sprinkle each cinnamon pinwheel with cinnamon-sugar mixture and drizzle with icing.

Serves 8.

Fried Bananas

Ingredients

Oil
1 cup cake flour
1 tablespoon granulated sugar
⅛ teaspoon salt
1 large egg
1 cup whipping cream
6 firm ripe bananas
2 cups fine dry bread crumbs
Powdered sugar
Easy Chocolate Sauce
    (see page 176)

COOKING INSTRUCTIONS

1 Preheat oil to 350°F.

2 In a small bowl combine flour, sugar, and salt; stir well with a whisk. In another bowl combine egg and cream; beat well with a whisk. Combine flour mixture and egg mixture; stir well.

3 Peel 1 banana. Cut in half crosswise; cut in half lengthwise. Dip banana pieces in batter. Dredge in bread crumbs, coating all sides well. Repeat procedure with remaining bananas.

4 Fry 5 or 6 pieces at a time for 3 minutes or until golden. Remove from hot oil and drain on paper towels. Dust with powdered sugar. Serve warm with Easy Chocolate Sauce.

Serves 12.

Deep Fried French Toast

Ingredients

Oil
2 13-ounce loaves French bread
8 large eggs
½ cup sugar
2 tablespoons milk
2 tablespoons vanilla
Powdered sugar

This is another version of an old French classic. It's perfect for breakfast, brunch, or a sweet ending to a delicious meal.

COOKING INSTRUCTIONS

1 Preheat oil to 350°F.

2 Cut bread on bias into 1-inch slices; discard end pieces. Combine eggs, sugar, milk, and vanilla; stir well with a whisk.

3 Dip 3 to 4 slices of bread into egg mixture. Fry 3 minutes or until golden brown, turning once. Remove from hot oil and drain on paper towels. Dust with powdered sugar. Serve warm.

Serves 8 to 10.

Real Easy Doughnuts

Ingredients

Oil
½ cup all-purpose flour
2 12-ounce packages refrigerated
buttermilk biscuits
2 cups sifted powdered sugar
½ cup milk

*You'd better eat some of these
while you're cooking, or there may
be none left by the time you finish.*

COOKING INSTRUCTIONS

I Preheat oil to 325°F.

2 On a clean cutting board or on a marble slab, sprinkle flour and rub into surface. Lightly sprinkle each biscuit with flour. Gently flatten each biscuit with palm of hand. Using a doughnut hole cutter or top of a small bottle, cut out center of each biscuit. Place doughnuts and holes on waxed paper sprinkled lightly with flour; set aside.

3 Combine powdered sugar and milk; stir well with a whisk until smooth.

4 Fry 4 or 5 doughnuts and holes at a time for 1½ to 2 minutes or until golden, turning once. Remove from hot oil and drain on paper towels. Dip tops of doughnuts and holes in glaze. Serve warm.

Serves 8 to 10.

FRYed Sweetness

Ingredients

1   8-ounce sweet potato
1   package active-dry yeast
1   cup warm buttermilk (105°F)
2   large eggs
2   tablespoons packed brown
     sugar
3½ cups all-purpose flour
1   teaspoon salt
½   teaspoon ground cinnamon
¼   teaspoon ground nutmeg
     Oil
     Apple Cider Glaze (see
       page 175)

*The flavor in this sweet fried pastry
comes from roasted sweet potatoes
and apple cider.*

COOKING INSTRUCTIONS

1 Preheat oven to 400°F.

2 Bake sweet potato for 1 hour. Remove from oven and cool completely. Spoon out pulp; discard jacket (sweet potato can be boiled until softened, if desired).

3 Sprinkle yeast over warm buttermilk; let stand 5 minutes. In a medium bowl combine eggs, brown sugar, and sweet potato pulp; stir well with a whisk until smooth.

4 In another bowl combine flour, salt, cinnamon, and nutmeg; stir with a whisk until mixture is free of lumps. Stir together sweet potato mixture and flour mixture until a soft dough forms; turn dough onto a lightly floured surface.

5 Knead just until dry ingredients are moistened. Do not overwork dough. Place in a greased bowl. Turn once to coat. Cover with a damp towel and let rise in a warm place free from drafts for 40 to 45 minutes or until double in size.

6 Turn dough onto a lightly floured surface; gently pat or roll to ½-inch thickness. Cut into doughnut rings or strips. Twist strips, if desired. Let rise for 30 minutes more, uncovered.

7 Preheat oil to 350°F.

8 Fry a few doughnuts at a time for 1 minute on each side or until golden. Remove from hot oil and drain on paper towels. Dip doughnuts in Apple Cider Glaze while hot. Serve immediately.

Serves 8.

Apple Cider Glaze

Ingredients

½ cup fresh apple cider, hard
   apple cider, or apple juice.
2 cups sifted powdered sugar

COOKING INSTRUCTIONS

Combine apple cider and powdered sugar; stir until smooth.

Makes 1 cup.

Easy Chocolate Sauce

Ingredients

- 1 6-ounce package semisweet chocolate pieces
- ¼ cup butter
- ½ cup light-colored corn syrup
- ¼ cup water
- 1 teaspoon vanilla
- 1 cup sifted powdered sugar

Pour this velvety sauce over fried bananas, dessert crêpes, or your favorite ice cream.

COOKING INSTRUCTIONS

1 Place chocolate pieces and butter in a 1-quart glass dish. Microwave on high 1 minute; stir. Microwave 1 minute more or until chocolate melts. Stir in corn syrup, water, and vanilla; microwave 1 minute more.

2 Add powdered sugar; stir until smooth.

Serves 12.

Chocolate-Cherry Sauce

Ingredients

1 12-ounce package semisweet chocolate pieces

1½ cups half-and-half

¾ cup prepared cherry frosting

COOKING INSTRUCTIONS

Combine chocolate pieces and half-and-half in a saucepan. Bring to a boil. Remove from heat; stir until chocolate melts. Add frosting; stir until smooth.

Makes about 3 cups.

Caramel Cream Sauce

Ingredients

1   12¼-ounce jar caramel topping
½   cup whipping cream
½   teaspoon vanilla extract
    Pinch of nutmeg

COOKING INSTRUCTIONS

Remove lid from jar of caramel topping. Microwave jar 45 seconds to 1 minute or until warm and pourable; pour into a bowl. Add cream, vanilla, and nutmeg; stir well.

Makes 2 cups.

Vanilla-Bourbon Sauce

Ingredients

1 pint vanilla ice cream

2 tablespoons bourbon or whiskey

¾ cup frozen whipped dessert topping, thawed

COOKING INSTRUCTIONS

Let ice cream stand at room temperature until fully melted. Add bourbon; stir well. Add whipped topping; stir with a whisk until smooth. Cover and chill 1 hour.

Makes about 2 cups.

Chapter 10
Favorites not FRYed

Creole Garlic Meat Loaf

Ingredients

- 3 pounds lean ground beef
- 1 onion, chopped
- 3 teaspoons minced garlic
- 1 tablespoon Chef Williams Original Cajun Seasoning
- 1 cup seasoned bread crumbs
- 2 eggs
- ½ cup milk
- 8 ounces Chef Williams Cajun Garlic Recipe

COOKING INSTRUCTIONS

1 Preheat oven to 350°F.

2 In a bowl combine meat, onion, garlic, Chef Williams Original Cajun Seasoning, bread crumbs, eggs, milk, and 2 ounces of the marinade.

3 Lightly pat mixture into a greased 8×4×2-inch loaf pan.

4 Inject 2 ounces of marinade into the center of the meat loaf; pour remaining 4 ounces over loaf.

5 Bake for 1 to 1½ hours or until internal temperature registers 160°F.

Serves 16.

Chicken in a Flash

Ingredients

1 2½- to 3-pound whole fryer
      chicken
   Chef Williams Cajun Butter
      Recipe
   Chef Williams Original Cajun
      Seasoning

*Add mixed vegetables to the
chicken for a complete, easy-on-
the-cook meal!*

COOKING INSTRUCTIONS

1 Remove giblets and neck; reserve for other uses.
   Rinse well with cold water; drain cavity. Dry well
with paper towels.

2 Using 1½ to 2 ounces marinade per pound of meat,
   inject marinade into several places in breasts,
thighs, and legs. Sprinkle with Chef Williams Original
Cajun Seasoning.

3 Microwave, covered, on high-heat setting 8 minutes
   per pound. Turn dish a quarter of a turn after half of
the cooking time. Remove chicken from microwave to
check for doneness. Insert an instant-read
thermometer in the meaty part of the thigh; chicken is
done when it reads 180°F.

Serves 4 to 6.

Favorites Not FRYed

Mama Jeanne's Seafood Gumbo

Ingredients

- 1 cup vegetable oil
- 1 cup flour
- 2 large yellow onions, chopped
- 4 stalks celery, chopped
- 1 14½-ounce can stewed tomatoes, undrained
- 4 quarts water or seafood stock
- Chef Williams Original Cajun Seasoning
- 3 pounds gumbo crabs, cut in half
- 2 pounds fresh or frozen shrimp, peeled and deveined
- 1 pound fresh or frozen lump crabmeat or claw meat
- 1 bunch green onions, chopped
- 1 cup fresh parsley, chopped
- 12 ounces shucked oysters, undrained (optional)
- Hot cooked rice

This recipe is sure to please! Make it ahead of time—it's even better the next day!

COOKING INSTRUCTIONS

1 To make a roux, cook oil and flour over medium heat in a heavy Dutch oven (black iron pot is even better). Stir the roux mixture constantly until dark brown. Do not burn.

2 Add yellow onions and cook for 5 minutes, stirring constantly. Add celery and stir another minute. Add stewed tomatoes and stir until combined.

3 Add water slowly; stir. Season to taste with Chef Williams Original Cajun Seasoning. Cook over medium heat for 30 minutes, adding more water or stock if necessary. Thaw crabs and shrimp, if frozen. Rinse seafood; pat dry with paper towels. Add crabs, shrimp, and crabmeat. Cook for 30 minutes. Fifteen minutes before serving, add green onions, parsley, and, if desired, undrained oysters.

4 Serve immediately over rice.

Serves 12.

Jeanne's Crabmeat au Gratin

Ingredients

- ¼ cup finely chopped onions
- 1 stalk celery, chopped
- 2 tablespoons butter
- ½ cup all-purpose flour
- 13 ounces evaporated milk
- 2 egg yolks
- 1 teaspoon salt
- ½ teaspoons Chef Williams Original Cajun Seasoning
- ¼ teaspoon black pepper
- 1 pound fresh or frozen lump crabmeat
- ½ pound grated sharp cheddar cheese

COOKING INSTRUCTIONS

Another award winning recipe. My mom won many cooking competitions with her crabmeat au gratin. In fact, I have never tasted one that compared.

1 Preheat oven to 375°F.

2 Cook and stir onions and celery in butter over medum heat until onions are tender. Stir in flour. Gradually add milk, stirring constantly. Add egg yolks, salt, Chef Williams Original Cajun Seasoning, and pepper; cook for 5 minutes.

3 Thaw crabmeat, if frozen. Rinse crabmeat; pat dry with paper towels. In a mixing bowl pour milk mixture over crabmeat. Gently fold together, being careful not to break up the crabmeat.

4 Transfer to a lightly greased casserole dish and sprinkle with cheese. Bake for 10 to 15 minutes or until heated through.

Serves 6.

Mary's Cajun Burgers

Ingredients

Lean ground beef

Chef Williams Cajun Garlic
    Recipe

Italian bread crumbs

Plan on ¼ to ⅓ pound of ground beef per person. Use 4 tablespoons marinade and 2 tablespoons bread crumbs per burger.

COOKING INSTRUCTIONS

My wife, Mary, has served this recipe to the kids and their friends for years. They always request these burgers when we are having a party.

In a bowl combine ground beef, marinade, and bread crumbs. Mold into patties and fry or grill until meat is no longer pink.

Serves as many as you like!

 186

My Sunday Pot Roast

Ingredients

1 5-pound beef rump roast
   Fresh garlic cloves, peeled and
      halved
   Chef Williams Original Cajun
      Seasoningor salt and black
      pepper
½ cup vegetable oil
½ cup all-purpose flour
   Water

*Every Sunday we looked forward to
Muma's pot roast, rice and gravy,
and English peas.*

COOKING INSTRUCTIONS

1 Cut several slits in roast with a small, sharp knife. Insert half of a garlic clove into each slit. Make as many slits as you like (the more garlic the better).

2 Rub the outside of roast with Chef Williams Original Cajun Seasoning, making sure that some gets into each of the slits.

3 Heat vegetable oil in a large skillet over medium heat. Brown meat on all sides. Remove from skillet and set aside.

4 To make a roux, add flour to the drippings left in the skillet. Cook over medium heat until roux is brown. Add roast back to skillet. Add enough water to cover the roast halfway. Cover and cook for 1½ to 2 hours or until internal temperature registers 160°F.

Serves 8 to 10.

Ingredients

1 8 pound boneless beef prime rib roast
20 ounces Chef Williams Cajun Garlic Recipe

Marinated prime rib is perfect for a dinner party. The mixture of spices and garlic in this marinade pairs perfectly with the rich flavor of the meat.

COOKING INSTRUCTIONS

This is the recipe my dad and I prepared when we first started serving meats injected with our marinade. The first recipe was made in 1979. In fact, when The Front Porch Restaurant won "Restaurant of the State" in 1979, this prime rib recipe was the featured recipe in all the restaurant news articles.

1 Preheat oven to 350°F.

2 Inject 16 ounces of marinade into meat in spots 1 to 2 inches apart. Pour remaining marinade over meat.

3 Place meat in a 15½×10½×2-inch roasting pan. Bake for 2¾ to 3hours or until internal temperature registers 155°F.

Serves 10 to 12.

Index

Index